The Farmer's Daughter Bakes

CAKES, PIES, CRISPS & MORE FOR EVERY FRUIT ON THE FARM

Kelsey Siemens

Creator of The Farmer's Daughter blog

PAGE STREET
PUBLISHING CO.

PAGE STREET
PUBLISHING CO.

Copyright © 2020 Kelsey Siemens

First published in 2020 by
Page Street Publishing Co.
27 Congress Street, Suite 105
Salem, MA 01970
www.pagestreetpublishing.com

Distributed by Macmillan, sales in Canada by The Canadian Manda Group.

24 23 22 21 20   1 2 3 4 5

ISBN-13: 978-1-64567-104-6
ISBN-10: 1-64567-104-6

Library of Congress Control Number: 2019957325

Cover and book design by Meg Baskis for Page Street Publishing Co.
Photography by Kelsey Siemens

Printed and bound in China

dedication

To my parents, for encouraging me to be brave in (and out of) the kitchen,
and to my sister, for being my biggest cheerleader.

To the readers of The Farmer's Daughter.

And to the farm, for giving me the best life I could ask for.

pie crusts 189

preserving the seasons 197

introduction

I am a child of farmers, who were children of farmers, and so on and so forth. From grain and cattle farming on the prairies, to dairy, then hogs and presently, apples. I guess you could say that farming is in my blood, and it was inevitable that I would find my way back home.

I grew up on a beautiful farm nestled in the fertile Fraser Valley of British Columbia, Canada. Willow View Farms. Named for the two enormous willow trees that stand guard at the entrance, as well as the stunning view we have of Mount Baker. My parents thought it was a good choice compared to using our last name . . . but I digress. The farm is home to around 10,000 dwarf apple trees, and we have roughly 20 acres of land at our home property. We grow over 50 varieties of pumpkins and squash, odd-looking gourds, the very best sweet corn, beautiful ornamental corn, a colorful array of potatoes, life-changing garlic, brilliantly red rhubarb and saskatoon berries. There was a time when we grew raspberries, blackberries and blueberries as well, but we've moved away from berry crops as our fall season grew in size and busyness.

It should come as no surprise that my life has been highly influenced by the seasons and the life of a farmer. Our livelihood is so tied into the land and its rhythms. We are forever watching the weather radar, checking in on our fields and holding on to faith that things will all work out. When will the rain come? When will it stop? Will the hail damage all our apple blossoms? Was the winter cold enough?

I worked on our farm growing up, as most farm kids do, and I am thankful for the way it shaped my work ethic and character. It started with small chores, collecting eggs and weeding in the garden, and eventually moved to working full-time during the summers. Pumpkin planting, hoeing, berry picking and orchard maintenance were all a huge part of my life. I learned how to drive a tractor at thirteen, with my dad just giving me a shrug and saying, "You can't hit anything in an empty field." When I graduated high school, I moved to the University of British Columbia to study . . . you guessed it, plants and soil. Summers were still spent at the farm, where I worked and saved money for the coming school year.

This is also when I started a food blog; my first recipe went live on July 7, 2010. It started out as a way to share recipes with friends and family, and it was a wonderful creative outlet as I soon fell in love with photography. Fast-forward a few years, and I'd graduated with a B.S. in geographical biogeosciences and gotten a job in a commercial greenhouse growing bell peppers. Taking pictures of food was now generating a tiny bit of income, and I was thrilled. Two years later, I came to the realization that I missed the farm. I missed working outside (although the greenhouse was close!), feeling the dirt on my hands and working with my family to grow our business. Luckily for me, my parents had both come to their own realizations about how much tougher things were without me and happily welcomed me back.

*   *   *

Eating seasonally comes naturally when you grow a lot of your own food. It's a privilege I don't take lightly. It feels like we can breathe again when the first green sprigs of fragrant herbs pop up in early spring. Biting into a piece of cake—still warm from the oven and packed with bright pink, deliciously tart rhubarb—is indescribable. Tree-ripened fruit, the way the fields smell during harvest, the satisfaction that comes from pulling things out of the ground with your own two hands. A warm pie, cooling on the counter, made with apples harvested that morning, nice and tart, please and thank you. These are a few of my favorite things.

This book starts in the spring, with rhubarb and strawberries stealing the show. Herbs and elderflowers make an appearance, lending their fresh flavors to loaves, cookies and bars. Summer is split into two parts: berries and the orchard. The berry chapter bursts with flavor, from a new spin on blueberry muffins (hint: we add lemon curd!) to an eye-catching bumbleberry pie made with a rye crust for some added wholesomeness. Then we walk through the orchard with cherries, peaches, plums and more, and I teach you what a *platz* is! Then we move to fall, my greatest love. Apples are front and center, as they should be, all things considered. Apple crisp layered over salted caramel cheesecake is pure heaven, and my sister makes a special appearance when she shares her pumpkin sourdough recipe. Winter caps things off with cozy flavors and hearty desserts. Chestnuts, cardamom, gingerbread and rosemary. Chocolate and caramel. And of course, citrus in several forms. The grapefruit-chili-lime tart (page 175) is one of the most unique recipes shared and adds a much needed bright spot during the darkest season.

Food simply tastes better when it's in season. Few things can top a perfectly ripe berry plucked straight from the field, the crunch of an apple on a cool fall morning or homemade pumpkin puree. These are the true stars, and I love keeping my recipes simple in a way that lets these flavors shine. Enjoying produce at its very best, waiting in anticipation for the next harvest and growing your own make you appreciate food in a new way.

My greatest wish is that this cookbook encourages you to connect with your local farmers, pick your own food when possible, visit fresh markets as often as you can and eat seasonally when you can. Be brave in the kitchen. Don't be afraid of making a mess—they're (almost) always worth it! Try something new, create new traditions and share with friends. Nothing would make me happier than to play a small part in all these things.

Kelsey Siemens

spring fever

Spring. It brings longer days, more sunshine and the promise of new life. It is one of a farmer's very favorite seasons, as the slow pace of winter fades away, and everything begins anew. Fields are prepped, seeds are planted and the trees blossom. Few things are more wondrous than walking through our orchard when the apple trees are bursting with flowers. Blossoms ranging from blush pink to pure white cover the recently bare branches, and the hum of worker bees fills the air. Buzzing. They fly slow and lazy, heavy with pollen, paying no mind to anything around them. And so, our own work begins. I often think of it as a journey of faith. Faith that our seeds will grow, our crops will flourish and all our hard work will pay off with a plentiful harvest in the coming months.

Spring is a time of renewal and preparation, and therefore its harvest is not overly robust. I find it the perfect time to utilize the last of my winter stores, frozen fruit and jams alike. Echoes of what the approaching season will bring. And then . . . herbs and flowers are the first to emerge. Sending up shoots of fresh flavor and opening colorful, fragrant petals as soon as the weather begins to warm. Mint and basil, lilacs and lavender, they all add such fresh flavor to complement many a dish. Whether infused into custard for Fresh Mint Nanaimo Bars (page 45) or baked into a fragrant Lavender-Lemon Loaf (page 41), they are a most welcome sight after winter's barren months.

Rhubarb is next. Tart and eye-catching, rhubarb holds such a dear place in my heart and is the star of many of my recipes. This ruby-red vegetable studs my great-grandmother's classic coffee cake (page 12) and is piped into pillowy soft Rhubarb-Filled Donuts Rolled in Lilac Sugar (page 19). Easy to grow in a backyard garden (although I'm lucky enough to have an entire field of it!), and so full of flavor, rhubarb is perfect to pair with many sweeter fruits. Coincidentally, strawberries arrive on the scene soon after. A match made in heaven. Their sweet burst of flavor comes later in the season . . . a hint to the summer berry bounty yet to come.

great-grandma enid's rhubarb-pistachio coffee cake

Every year, as soon as our rhubarb is just barely tall enough to harvest (I will check the field daily as my anticipation for the season to start is always exceptionally high!), my mom makes this coffee cake. It doesn't feel like spring has officially started until I walk into her kitchen and am enveloped in the cozy smell of cinnamon and sugar and rhubarb goodness. The recipe has been passed down from her grandma, and is a family favorite. I added pistachios to my version, but it's also lovely with almonds or simply left plain.

Yield: 1 round 9-inch (23-cm) cake or 1 rectangular 9 x 13–inch (23 x 33–cm) cake

CAKE

1 cup (240 ml) milk

1 tbsp (15 ml) white vinegar or lemon juice

½ cup (114 g) unsalted butter, room temperature

1½ cups (330 g) packed brown sugar

1 large egg

1 tsp vanilla extract

2¼ cups (281 g) all-purpose flour

1 tsp baking soda

1½ cups (150 g) chopped rhubarb, ½" (1.3-cm) pieces

¼ cup (25 g) roughly chopped pistachios or almonds (optional)

½ rhubarb stalk, cut into thin slices about ⅛" (3 mm) thick and 3–4" (8–10 cm) long (optional)

TOPPING

¼ cup (50 g) granulated sugar

1 tsp cinnamon

FOR SERVING

Powdered sugar (optional)

Preheat the oven to 350°F (180°C). Grease a 9-inch (23-cm) round springform pan (alternatively, use a greased 9 x 13–inch [23 x 33–cm] baking dish) and set aside.

To make the cake, in a small bowl, mix the milk with the vinegar and let stand for 5 minutes. This creates a sour milk, which is used below. Set aside.

In the bowl of a stand mixer fitted with the paddle attachment, cream together the butter and sugar on medium for 3 to 4 minutes. Add the egg and vanilla and mix on medium-low until the mixture is light and fluffy. Add the sour milk and mix on low until combined. Gradually add the flour and baking soda and mix on medium-low until just combined. Fold in the rhubarb pieces with a spatula, and be sure to scrape down the sides and bottom of the bowl.

To make the topping, in a small bowl combine the sugar and cinnamon.

Pour the batter into the prepared pan, and top with the cinnamon and sugar mixture. Sprinkle the pistachios around the outer edge, if using. Arrange the rhubarb slices on top, if using. Bake for 50 to 60 minutes, or until an inserted toothpick comes out clean. Allow to cool for 5 minutes before running a knife around the edge of the cake and carefully removing the outside of the spring-form pan. For a 9 x 13–inch (23 x 33–cm) pan, reduce the baking time to 30 to 35 minutes, and let the cake cool in the pan. This cake is best served warm on the same day, topped with powdered sugar directly before serving, if using.

Note: You can replace the cinnamon-sugar mixture with powdered sugar if you'd like.

Seasonal Substitutes

This coffee cake is incredibly versatile, and strawberries, blueberries or diced apples all work well in place of the rhubarb.

rhubarb-lemon layer cake

As a small child, my spring afternoons were spent in the rhubarb field, playing on a blanket while my parents harvested the crop beside me. They would hand me a small stalk to keep me occupied, and I would happily munch away! It's a running joke in my family that when I'm in a sour mood, it's due to the sour rhubarb I ate as a child. This cake combines my love for all things tart with light, lemon cake layers, a beautifully pink rhubarb compote and dreamy frosting. Play around with the compote's sweetness, depending on your own preference. I prefer it on the tart side, as it balances the cake and frosting well. Extra rhubarb compote is perfect for serving on ice cream, overnight oats and more!

Yield: 1 round 6-inch (15-cm) three-layer cake

LEMON CAKE

¾ cup (180 ml) egg whites (about 6 eggs)

2 tsp (10 ml) vanilla extract

¾ cup (180 ml) milk, divided

2 cups (240 g) cake flour

1 cup (125 g) all-purpose flour

1½ cups (300 g) granulated sugar

1 tbsp (14 g) baking powder

2 tbsp (12 g) lemon zest (about 2 lemons)

½ tsp salt

1 cup (240 ml) canola oil

¼ cup (60 ml) plain, full-fat Greek yogurt or regular plain, full-fat yogurt

To make the cake, preheat the oven to 350°F (180°C). Grease three round 6-inch (15-cm) cake pans with straight, 2-inch (5-cm) sides and set aside. In a small bowl, whisk the egg whites, vanilla extract and ¼ cup (60 ml) of the milk and set aside. In the bowl of a stand mixer fitted with the paddle attachment, mix the cake flour, all-purpose flour, sugar, baking powder, lemon zest and salt on low until combined. Add the oil, remaining milk and Greek yogurt and mix on low until just moistened. Scrape down the sides and bottom of the bowl with a spatula, and then turn the mixer to medium-high and mix until completely combined.

With your mixer on medium-low, slowly stream in the egg white and milk mixture. Add it in three batches, where each addition should take about 15 seconds to stream in. Ensure each batch is completely incorporated before adding the next. Stop the mixer before the last addition is completely incorporated and finish mixing by hand, using a spatula to fold together, scraping down the sides and bottom of the bowl as you go. Try not to overmix at this point! Distribute the batter among the prepared pans. I like to use a kitchen scale to make sure an even amount is in each one, but you can just eyeball it. Bake for 25 to 30 minutes or until a toothpick inserted into the center of the cakes comes out clean. I also like to carefully rotate my pans a couple of times while cooking to ensure even heating. Allow the cakes to cool for at least 5 to 10 minutes before removing from the pans and cooling completely on a cooling rack. Use a large, serrated knife to level the tops of each one before assembling the layer cake.

Make the rhubarb compote while the cake is baking, and let it cool to room temperature before using.

(continued)

½ cup (120 ml) egg whites
(about 4 eggs)

1 cup (200 g) granulated sugar

Pinch of salt

1 tsp vanilla extract

1¼ cups (284 g) cubed unsalted
butter, room temperature

½–¾ cup (120–180 ml) Rhubarb
Compote (page 207), room
temperature

FOR ASSEMBLY

⅔ cup (160 ml) Rhubarb Compote
(page 207), room temperature

Fresh flowers (optional)

Sprinkles or piped frosting
(optional)

Note: If you choose a
smooth finish, you may
have leftover frosting. Keep
in an airtight container in
the freezer until you need it.

To make the rhubarb swiss meringue frosting, prepare a double boiler by filling a medium-large saucepan with a few inches of water and bringing it to a simmer. In a metal bowl that will sit on top of the saucepan without touching the water, place the egg whites and sugar and whisk together until just combined. Keep stirring the mixture occasionally, and cook until the sugar is completely dissolved and the temperature hits 160°F (71°C). Don't whisk vigorously here, or you'll start forming your meringue prematurely. Remove from the heat once it reaches temperature and pour it into the bowl of a stand mixer fitted with the whisk attachment. Beat the mixture for 7 to 8 minutes on high or until it has cooled to room temperature and forms shiny, medium-stiff peaks.

Switch to the paddle attachment, then add the salt and vanilla extract. With the mixer on low, add the butter 1 tablespoon (14 g) at a time. Mix well after each addition. This is where problems may occur if the meringue isn't cooled down enough or if the butter is too cold, etc (see Frosting Troubleshooting, page 18). Stir in the rhubarb compote ¼ cup (60 ml) at a time, watching carefully for curdling or separation. I usually add ¾ cup (180 ml) into mine since I like a strong rhubarb flavor, but if the compote is too runny, the juices may cause the buttercream to separate and it may not be reparable.

Store the frosting in an airtight container in the fridge (or freezer) if you're not using it right away! Let it sit on the counter to soften up before icing a cake with it. You may need to re-whip it for a few minutes to get its smooth texture back.

To assemble the cake, place the first layer upside down onto your cake plate (this reduces the number of crumbs as the cut part is facedown). Spread the frosting in an even layer, but come up slightly along the edge of the cake layer to create a small barrier for the compote. I use about 2 scoops of frosting from a 2½-inch (6-cm) ice cream scoop between each cake layer so that I know my frosting layers will be even. Next, spread a layer of the rhubarb compote on top of the frosting. Use 1 or 1½ scoops from the ice cream scoop (about ⅓ cup [80 ml] of compote). Repeat for the next layer. When the final cake layer is placed on top (remember to place it upside down to reduce crumbs), spread a very thin layer of frosting over the entire cake as your crumb coat. Now is a good time to check how straight your cake is standing and gently adjust the layers if possible so that it's standing straight. I like to place my cake scraper (also called an icing smoother) along one side and push from the other side to get it perfectly level. Move the cake into the fridge or freezer for 10 to 15 minutes to firm up.

(continued)

Note: Chilled cake layers are easier to handle, and you'll have fewer crumbs in your icing. I like to make the cakes the day (or even week) before, store them in an airtight container and keep them in the fridge or freezer to keep fresh. If storing cake layers in your freezer, remove and place in your fridge 3 to 4 hours before assembly, or overnight, to let them thaw before frosting.

To frost the cake, scoop more frosting onto the chilled crumb layer, and use a cake scraper to smooth out the frosting as you turn the cake. Or you can keep it more rustic and swirly and have a thicker layer of frosting.

I love using flowers from the garden to decorate cakes. Place plastic wrap where the flowers will go, wrap flower stems with floral tape and use floral wire to help arrange the blooms. Remove the flowers and plastic wrap before serving. Alternatively, decorate with sprinkles, piped frosting, etc. Cut in slices and serve. Store any leftover cake in the fridge or freezer in an airtight container.

Seasonal Substitutes

Swap most other fruit compotes in for the rhubarb. A citrus curd would also be lovely (see page 208 for a lemon curd recipe).

Frosting Troubleshooting

Swiss meringue frosting can be fussy, so here are some tips!

- Our goal temperature for the frosting is about 72 to 74°F (22 to 23°C). I learned this tip from Stella Parks and swear by it! The meringue should be cooled to about 90°F (32°C) before adding any butter. The butter should be about 65°F (18°C) before adding it to the meringue, otherwise it may turn lumpy and curdled.

- Soupy meringue? Simply place it back into the fridge for about 15 to 20 minutes, and then re-whip for a full 4 minutes, and it should come together. Seriously . . . just keep whipping!

- Lumpy or curdled meringue? It may look thick or even weirdly thin and separating, but in both instances, you actually need to heat it up a little. Place the bowl back on the double boiler and heat until the frosting starts to melt a little on the sides of the bowl. Place the bowl back in the stand mixer and whip for another 4 minutes.

rhubarb-filled donuts rolled in lilac sugar

Lilacs feel like spring's herald, announcing the season's arrival with color and fragrance. My mom has several wild bushes in shades of purple (both light and dark) and white, just begging to be picked and enjoyed for a few short weeks in spring. Lilac sugar is delightfully delicate and adds a depth to these donuts that is truly lovely. A slightly tart rhubarb compote is piped inside fluffy round donuts to provide the perfect balance for this sweet treat. As with most donuts, these are best served fresh.

Yield: approximately 12 donuts

½ tbsp (5 g) active dry yeast

¼ cup (50 g) granulated sugar, divided

¼ cup (60 ml) hot water

2 tbsp (28 g) shortening, room temperature

1 cup (240 ml) buttermilk, room temperature

1 large egg, room temperature

½ tsp salt

4–4¼ cups (500–531 g) all-purpose flour

Canola or other neutral oil, for frying

Lilac Sugar (page 198) or plain sugar, to taste

Rhubarb Compote (page 207), as needed

Note: The lilac sugar in this recipe will need to be made several days in advance; however, regular sugar will work just fine in its stead.

In a small bowl, combine the yeast, ½ teaspoon of the sugar and the hot (but not boiling) water. Let it rise for about 5 minutes. If this mixture doesn't get nice and foamy, discard and try again to ensure the yeast is active. Set aside. In the bowl of a stand mixer fitted with the whisk attachment, mix the remaining sugar, shortening, buttermilk and the egg on medium until smooth, 1 to 2 minutes. Add the foamy yeast mixture and mix on low until incorporated. Switch to the dough hook and add the salt and 4 cups (500 g) of flour to start, mixing on low. Continue mixing, adding more flour by the tablespoon (8 g) until the dough pulls away from the sides of the bowl and forms a ball. The dough should still be a bit tacky, so try not to add more flour than you need to. If using a stand mixer, allow to mix on low for 5 minutes. If using a handheld mixer, switch to kneading by hand, and knead for 8 to 10 minutes.

Place the dough in a clean, greased bowl, cover with a clean dish towel and place in a warm spot for about 1 hour or until the dough has doubled. Roll out the dough to a thickness of ½ inch (1.3 cm). Use a round cookie cutter to cut out donut shapes. Mine was 3 inches (7.5 cm) in diameter, but you can choose whatever size you like. Place the donuts onto a parchment-lined cookie sheet, cover with a clean dish towel and let rise for about 30 minutes. You'll know the donuts are ready to fry when you press your fingertip into one and the indentation stays. About 20 minutes into the rise time, begin heating the oil. There should be enough oil that the donuts will float about 2 inches (5 cm) above the bottom, while being about half immersed. You will also want to set up a wire rack directly beside the fryer and line it with paper towels to absorb excess oil.

Once the oil is heated to about 375°F (190°C) (it's normal for the temperature to fluctuate a bit while you fry), carefully place a donut in to test your cook time. After 45 seconds of frying time, carefully check the first side. If it's golden brown, flip it. If not, let it go for 15 to 20 seconds. Repeat for the other side. Remove the donut using a slotted spoon or spider strainer and place onto the wire rack. Allow to cool for 1 minute and immediately roll in the lilac sugar. The donuts should be fully cooked within 2 to 3 minutes.

(continued)

Note: A deep fryer works best, although I've used an electric frying pan for many years as well. These both control the temperature for you, and I find them safer and easier to use compared to using a pot on the stove. If you use a pot on the stove, make sure it's a heavy-bottomed one, which will absorb and distribute heat more evenly and help keep the temperature steady. You will need a candy/deep fryer thermometer on hand to keep an eye on the temperature.

Cut open your first test donut to check for doneness. If your oil is too hot, it can cause your donut to brown too quickly while leaving the middle raw. If the oil is not hot enough, the donut will soak up more oil while cooking more slowly. This can result in a greasy donut. You may need to adjust your oil temperature. Repeat the frying process for all the donuts. You may be able to fry several at once depending on your frying vessel of choice; just use caution as this can cause the temperature to drop quite a bit if overloaded. Once all the donuts are fried, use a small paring knife or the handle of a wooden spoon to poke a hole into each one and wiggle the knife or spoon handle around to create a cavity for the rhubarb compote to go into.

Place the rhubarb compote into a large pastry bag fitted with a small, round tip. Hold a donut in one hand with the hole you've made facing up. Pipe the compote into the donut, filling it as full as you can. You will feel the donut get heavier in your hand, and a little compote will come out the top when it's full. Repeat with all of the remaining donuts. Serve immediately. These donuts are best the same day they are made.

Seasonal Substitutes

These donuts may be filled with any fruit compote your heart desires and are wonderful all year round. Any flavor-infused sugar works here, or even just regular granulated sugar. Try adding freeze-dried berry powder for an extra kick of flavor!

rhubarb mini pies with spelt crust

To propagate a rhubarb plant, you can simply dig it up and cut it into pieces. We have multiplied our rhubarb fields many times over the years, and it's tough work! Yielding a machete and repeatedly chopping up 4-foot (1.2-m)-wide chunks of rhubarb roots is a great way to work out any frustrations you have, let me tell ya. The best fuel for such hard work is always pie. I love adding a little spelt flour to my crust for a delicate touch of nuttiness, and it never weighs the flaky dough down! Combined with the fresh, tart flavor of rhubarb, these mini pies are a dream.

Yield: 4 (4-inch [10-cm]) double-crust mini pies

4 cups (400 g) chopped rhubarb, ½" (1.3-cm) pieces (about 4 stalks)

1⅓ cups (266 g) granulated sugar

1 tsp ground cinnamon

¼ cup (31 g) all-purpose flour

1 batch Pie Dough with spelt flour variation (page 191)

TOPPING

1 large egg, lightly beaten

1 tbsp (15 ml) heavy cream or milk

Coarse sugar, as needed

FOR SERVING

Ice cream or cream (optional)

In a large mixing bowl, toss the rhubarb, sugar, cinnamon and flour. Set aside. Remove one disk of pie crust dough from the fridge and cut it into 4 equal pieces. On a lightly floured surface, roll each piece of dough into a circle about ⅛ inch (3 mm) thick. Place each piece of dough into a mini pie plate, leaving a ½-inch (1.3-cm) border hanging over the edge of the plate. Fill each pie shell with about 1 cup (240 ml) of the prepared rhubarb filling, or until the pie dish is full.

Remove a second pie crust dough disk from the fridge and repeat the above process. Use a small cookie cutter to cut out small vent holes, or cut the dough into strips to create a lattice. Place each dough circle on top of each pie, and trim the edges if needed so that they are even. Use a fork to firmly press the crust together along the edges. Move all the pies onto a medium baking sheet and place in the freezer for 15 minutes, or until the crusts are firm to the touch.

While the pies are chilling, preheat the oven to 400°F (200°C).

To make the topping, in a small bowl, mix the egg and heavy cream. Set aside.

Remove the baking sheet with the pies from the freezer, brush the tops with the egg wash using a pastry brush and sprinkle generously with coarse sugar. Bake the pies for 15 minutes, and then reduce the oven temperature to 350°F (180°C). Bake for 15 to 20 minutes, or until the crust is deep golden brown and the filling is visibly bubbling. Cool the pies before serving so that the filling doesn't run everywhere. Serve with ice cream or a splash of cream.

Note: I used 4-inch (10-cm) tart pans with removable bottoms, but you can use any small pie plates you have on hand or even a muffin tin; although, the crust-to-filling ratio might differ slightly.

rhubarb-raspberry crisp

If you've ever picked more than a few stalks of rhubarb at once, you'll be familiar with the distinct purple color staining your nails! Mine are constantly purple-hued during harvest time, and I honestly don't mind. When picking rhubarb, you want your stalks to be at least 10 to 15 inches (25 to 38 cm) long (although ours tend to grow even longer in our growing conditions!). They should snap easily if you were to crack one in half (no bendy-ness, please), and you should never harvest more than two-thirds of the plant at one time. Grasp each stalk firmly at the base, and slowly pull upwards, twisting slightly as you go. We grow a beautiful red variety, which makes for eye-catching, vibrant desserts. Rhubarb pairs well with so many varieties of berries, and this crisp is easily customizable with whatever fruit you have on hand. Simply stir together the fruit, sugar and a dash of cinnamon; layer with a simple crumb topping; and bake. Best served warm with a big scoop of ice cream.

Yield: 1 (8 x 8-inch [20 x 20-cm]) crisp

CRUMB TOPPING

⅓ cup (41 g) all-purpose flour

½ tsp baking powder

½ cup (45 g) rolled oats

⅛ tsp salt

¼ tsp ground ginger

¼ cup (57 g) butter, cold

FRUIT FILLING

3–4 cups (300–400 g) chopped rhubarb, ½" (1.3-cm) pieces

½–¾ cup (100–150 g) granulated sugar

1 tbsp (8 g) all-purpose flour

½ tsp ground cinnamon

1–2 cups (123–246 g) fresh or frozen raspberries

Note: Use more or less fruit depending on your ideal fruit-to-crumb-layer ratio! I love more fruit, so I usually choose to use the higher end of the measurements.

Preheat the oven to 350°F (180°C). Grease an 8 x 8–inch (20 x 20–cm) pan and set aside.

To make the crumb topping, in a medium bowl, stir together the flour, baking powder, rolled oats, salt and ground ginger. Slice the chilled butter into ½-inch (1.3-cm) cubes, and cut into the flour mixture with a pastry cutter or fork until it resembles coarse crumbs. Move to the fridge while you prepare the fruit.

To make the fruit filling, in a large bowl, stir the rhubarb, sugar, flour and cinnamon together with a spatula or wooden spoon. Pour roughly two-thirds of the rhubarb mixture into the prepared pan, spread the raspberries on top and finish with the rest of the rhubarb. This keeps the raspberries from becoming mush during the mixing process. Evenly sprinkle the crumbs over the fruit.

Bake for 35 to 45 minutes, or until the crumbs are golden brown and the fruit is tender. Serving it warm is my preferred method; just be warned that it may be a bit runny until it completely cools.

Seasonal Substitutes

Swap strawberries or blueberries in place of the raspberries or use apples in place of the rhubarb. I would scale back the sugar if using a sweeter fruit than the original recipe.

roasted strawberry and rhubarb pavlova with elderflower-infused whipped cream

There is nothing quite like the taste of a perfectly ripe strawberry picked fresh off the vine, especially after the barren winter months. Our local strawberries are usually a little smaller, a lot redder and intensely more flavorful than the varieties that are stocked in grocery stores all year round. And the smell of the fields? Pure heaven. There's a sweet farm up the road from us that opens their fields to u-pick in the spring and summer months, letting visitors come with buckets to fill to the brim. I always pick some to eat fresh as well as a mountain to freeze for the rest of the year. When I want to bring out even more of their flavor? I roast them. Trust me when I say that roasting elevates the taste even further, as it does with roasted rhubarb. Pair with a crunchy-on-the-outside, marshmallowy-on-the-inside pavlova, and top with an elderflower whipped cream, and you have a trifecta of spring flavors all in one dessert.

Yield: 1 (9-inch [23-cm]) pavlova

MERINGUE

½ cup (120 ml) egg whites (about 4 large eggs)

⅛ tsp cream of tartar

1 cup (200 g) granulated sugar

2 tsp (10 ml) lemon juice

1 tsp vanilla extract

½ tbsp (4 g) cornstarch

ROASTED RHUBARB AND STRAWBERRIES

2 cups (304 g) halved strawberries

2½ cups (250 g) sliced rhubarb, ¼" x 2" (6-mm x 5-cm) slices

2–3 tbsp (30–45 g) granulated sugar

To make the meringue, preheat the oven to 300°F (150°C). Line a large baking sheet with parchment paper and set aside.

In the bowl of a stand mixer fitted with the whisk attachment, beat the egg whites with the cream of tartar on medium-high until soft peaks start to form. Add the sugar 1 tablespoon (15 g) at a time, until it's fully incorporated. Turn the speed to high and whip until the meringue forms stiff and shiny peaks, about 6 to 8 minutes. Use a spatula to gently fold in the lemon juice, vanilla extract and cornstarch, being careful not to deflate the pavlova mixture. Carefully spread the meringue onto the parchment paper and form a 9-inch (23-cm) circle. The middle should be slightly concave with the sides coming up a bit higher.

Place the baking sheet into the oven, and reduce the oven temperature to 250°F (120°C). Bake for about 1 hour or until it is a very light cream color. Turn off the oven, leave the door cracked open and allow to cool completely in the oven for at least 1 hour. Store in an airtight container at room temperature for up to 2 days. It also keeps wonderfully in an airtight container in the freezer, no need to thaw before serving.

To roast the fruit, preheat the oven to 375°F (190°C). Place the halved strawberries and rhubarb pieces into a glass 9 x 13–inch (23 x 33–cm) baking dish, and sprinkle evenly with 2 to 3 tablespoons (30 to 45 g) of sugar. Roast for 15 to 20 minutes, stirring occasionally, until soft and juicing. Set aside to cool. Reserve the juice to drizzle over the pavlova or keep to serve over ice cream.

(continued)

roasted strawberry and rhubarb pavlova
with elderflower-infused whipped cream (continued)

ELDERFLOWER WHIPPED
CREAM

1 cup (240 ml) whipping cream

1 tbsp (15 ml) Elderflower Cordial
(page 201), or to taste

FOR SERVING

Fresh mint leaves, chopped
(optional)

To make the elderflower whipped cream, place the whipping cream in the bowl of a stand mixer fitted with the whisk attachment and whip on high until soft peaks form. Add the elderflower cordial to taste, and whip until stiff peaks form. (Alternatively, sweeten with powdered sugar and flavor with vanilla.)

Immediately before serving, top the meringue with the whipped cream and pile high with the roasted fruit. Cut and serve topped with fresh mint leaves, if desired. Refrigerate any leftovers in an airtight container for a day or two, but it is best the day it is made.

Seasonal Substitutes

Swap in your choice of fresh (or roasted) fruit, citrus curd or even add chocolate, caramel and nuts.

strawberry-elderflower ice cream

Elderflowers are such a treasure, with their sweet, floral smell and beautiful, cream-colored, flat-headed sprays made up of hundreds of tiny blossoms. Elder trees are often found in gardens, but they also grow wild. It's very important that you're able to identify elder trees properly if you do decide to go foraging! We have quite a large tree growing on the corner of one of our fields, and I anxiously count the days until it blossoms in spring. It's a common sight to see our tractor full of fresh-picked blossoms as I make my way back from working the fields, happy as can be with their scent filling the air around me. Then they are trimmed and placed on a baking sheet covered by a damp cloth until I'm ready to use them. Elderflowers pair well with strawberries, as they add a delicately floral hint to this dessert. I chose a Philadelphia-style ice cream (no egg yolks!), so that the flavors could truly shine. Simply heat the sugar, milk and cream together to help the sugar dissolve, and stir in the cordial and blended strawberries. The ice cream maker does the rest of the work!

Yield: 5 cups (680 g) of ice cream

1½ cups (228 g) halved strawberries

1 tbsp (15 g) granulated sugar

1½ cups (360 ml) whipping cream

1 cup (240 ml) whole milk

½ cup (120 ml) Elderflower Cordial (page 201)

Preheat the oven to 375°F (180°C).

Place the halved strawberries on a rimmed 10 x 15–inch (25 x 38–cm) baking sheet and sprinkle with the sugar. Roast for 15 to 20 minutes, stirring occasionally, until soft and juicing. Set aside to cool. Reserve the juice to drizzle over the ice cream. In a large bowl, stir together the cream, milk and elderflower cordial. Place the strawberries in a blender and blend until mostly smooth. Add the strawberry puree to the cream mixture. Test for sweetness and add more cordial if needed, as strawberries and personal preferences vary.

Pour the mixture into your ice cream maker and follow your machine's instructions. I churn mine for about 20 to 30 minutes, until the ice cream is quite thick. Serve immediately as soft serve or place in an airtight container and move to the freezer to firm up for a couple of hours. This ice cream is at its best within the first few days after making it. As it sits in the freezer, it will get harder and may need 10 to 15 minutes on the counter to make scooping it easier.

strawberry galette

Strawberries were the first berry that I learned to love. I was a bit of a fussy kid with fruit, but local strawberries helped set me straight with their sweet, unintimidating flavor and juicy texture. Ironically, it was also one of the few berries we didn't grow on our farm for very long, as my parents gave up after a few years of frustration. We keep things simple for this galette, letting the strawberries truly shine. Flaky pie dough, a dash of sweetness and a touch of lemon zest are all that's needed for this spring essential.

Yield: 1 round 10-inch (25-cm) galette

GALETTE

½ batch Pie Dough (page 191), chilled

3 cups (456 g) halved strawberries

2–4 tbsp (30–60 g) granulated sugar, depending on the strawberries' sweetness

1 tsp vanilla extract

1 tsp lemon zest

TOPPING

1 large egg, beaten

1 tbsp (15 ml) milk or cream

Coarse sugar, as desired

Preheat the oven to 425°F (220°C). Line a 13 x 18–inch (33 x 46–cm) rimmed baking sheet with parchment paper and set aside.

To make the galette, on a lightly floured surface, roll out the chilled pie dough into a rough 14-inch (36-cm) circle. Trim the edge smooth, if desired. Carefully drape the dough over the rolling pin, transfer onto the prepared baking sheet and move to the fridge if the dough feels like it's getting soft. We want the dough to stay cold but not to be too stiff when we fold the edges up. Otherwise it may crack. In a large bowl, stir together the strawberry halves, sugar, vanilla and lemon zest with a spatula. Spread the mixture onto the prepared pie dough, leaving about a 2-inch (5-cm) border around the edge. Working with 3 to 4 inches (8 to 10 cm) of length at a time, fold the edge of the dough up over the strawberry mixture, pressing the seams together where they overlap. Repeat until all the edges are folded up. Place the galette in the freezer for 10 to 15 minutes, or until the dough is very firm.

To make the topping, in a small bowl, whisk together the egg and milk.

Remove the galette from the freezer and brush the edges of the dough with the egg mixture. This helps give the crust a beautiful golden shine. Sprinkle with coarse sugar, if using, and immediately place in the oven. Bake for 30 to 40 minutes, or until the crust is golden and the filling is starting to bubble. Cool slightly and serve.

Seasonal Substitutes

Blueberries, peach slices or cubed apples work wonderfully in this galette.

vertical purple carrot cake with mascarpone frosting

Have you ever pulled a carrot out of the ground? It puts all grocery store carrots to shame. Growing up, I was expected to help my mom keep the weeds down in the veggie garden. She grew rows of carrots and kale, broccoli and beans, snap peas and sunflowers. My sister and I would be assigned our own rows, and we'd race to see who finished first. Carrots were perhaps the most fun. Careful consideration of which leafy top was the largest was a given, and then we would grab, pull and behold our bounty. A quick rinse with the hose, and then we would chomp down. Sweet, tender and delicious. Nothing beats a garden carrot.

This cake is similar to a jelly roll cake, except the roll sits upright, creating vertical layers. It is so fun to cut into it in front of an audience and see them marvel at how you managed to get the layers to sit up and down. Be sure to give yourself lots of time to let this cake cool down and then chill! It's best made the day before you'd like to serve it.

Yield: 1 round 7-inch (18-cm) cake

CAKE

6 large eggs

1 cup (220 g) packed brown sugar

⅔ cup (132 g) granulated sugar

2 tsp (10 ml) vanilla extract

1 tsp ground ginger

⅛ tsp ground nutmeg

¼ tsp salt

2 tsp (9 g) baking soda

¼ tsp baking powder

1½ cups (188 g) all-purpose flour

2 cups (220 g) shredded purple carrot (any color carrot will work)

Preheat the oven to 350°F (180°C). Line two 9 x 13–inch (23 x 33–cm) rimmed baking sheets with parchment paper, ensuring there is a 1-inch (2.5-cm) border of excess along each side. Lightly grease the parchment paper with cooking oil and set aside.

To make the cake, in the bowl of a stand mixer fitted with the whisk attachment, whip the eggs on medium-high speed, and slowly add the sugars a few tablespoons at a time. Add the vanilla extract. It will form a thick and foamy mixture and will take 1 to 2 minutes. In a separate large bowl, whisk together the ginger, nutmeg, salt, baking soda, baking powder and flour. With the mixer on medium-low, slowly add the dry ingredients to the egg mixture and mix until almost combined. Remove the bowl from the stand mixer, and use a spatula to fold in the shredded carrots and to finish mixing the batter. Mix until just combined. The batter will be thin and pourable.

Divide the batter between the prepared baking sheets, and spread each one into an even layer. Bake for 13 to 15 minutes, or until golden and an inserted toothpick comes out clean. Remove the cakes from the oven and carefully lift each one off its baking sheet (still attached to the parchment paper) and onto a cooling rack.

(continued)

vertical purple carrot cake with mascarpone frosting (continued)

MASCARPONE FROSTING

1 cup (232 g) mascarpone, room temperature

1 cup (227 g) unsalted butter, room temperature

2–3 cups (240–360 g) powdered sugar

1 tsp vanilla extract

Milk or cream, if needed to adjust consistency

FOR SERVING

Fresh flowers (optional)

Sprinkles (optional)

Working carefully, start with the short side and roll each cake up, keeping the parchment attached so the cake doesn't stick to itself. Careful though, the cake will be hot! It's important you do this before the cake has cooled too much, otherwise it will simply crack as you roll. When you've finished rolling each log, it will look like the parchment is the filling to the roll. That's just right. Let the cakes cool completely before assembling with the frosting. This will take a few hours.

Once the cake is almost done cooling, prepare the frosting. In the bowl of a stand mixer fitted with the paddle attachment, add the mascarpone and butter. Mix on medium-high until the mixture is pale and fluffy, about 2 to 3 minutes. With the mixer on low, slowly add 2 cups (240 g) of the powdered sugar and the vanilla extract. Increase the speed to medium and mix until completely smooth. Adjust the consistency with more powdered sugar or a splash of milk, if needed. The frosting should be smooth and thick enough that it is stable when the cake is rolled.

Once the cake rolls have completely cooled and the frosting is made, you can start assembling the vertical cake. These steps may seem a bit tricky, but once you start, it will make more sense! Very carefully, unroll one of the cake logs. It will likely want to stay a bit curled up, and you may experience a little cracking—that's normal! Spread a generous layer of frosting onto the cake.

With the short edge closest to you, use a knife or pizza cutter to cut the cake in half, creating two long strips, each about 5 inches (13 cm) wide and 15 inches (38 cm) long.

Roll up one of the halves. Place the half in the middle of a cake plate. Carefully pick up the second half and place one of its edges exactly where the first log's edge ended, and wrap the cake around the first rolled section. Repeat with the second cake.

If any of the pieces crack as you're working, simply use more frosting to piece it together. When you reach the end of the last cake strip, you may want to shave off the end a bit to help it blend into the rest of the cake better, and not be an abrupt edge. This will be more obvious once you're at this step with your cake.

Frost the cake with the remaining frosting.

You may want to chill the cake in the freezer for 10 to 15 minutes before doing this if it seems a bit wobbly. Decorate with fresh flowers, if desired, placing down a bit of plastic wrap or cardboard topped with frosting where the flowers will go and wrapping the flower ends with floral tape. Or simply use sprinkles or candles. Once frosted, chill the entire cake in the fridge for a couple of hours before serving.

lavender shortbread cookies

It shouldn't come as a surprise that despite growing things for a living, my mom's favorite hobby is gardening. The same goes for my grandma. I've inherited their love for plants, whether it be pumpkins or peonies. Spring is always such an exciting time of year as the year's first flowers appear. Lavender offers a soft, fragrant touch to these melt-in-your-mouth shortbread cookies. Confession: I almost always use salted butter in my everyday baking, and I recommend it for these cookies! If that makes you nervous, simply use unsalted, and add ¼ teaspoon of salt.

Yield: approximately 20 cookies

1 tbsp (5 g) dried culinary-grade lavender

¼ cup (50 g) granulated sugar

¼ cup (55 g) packed brown sugar

1 cup (227 g) salted butter, room temperature

2⅓ cups (291 g) all-purpose flour

Coarse sugar, as needed (optional)

Preheat the oven to 325°F (165°C). Line a 10 x 15–inch (25 x 38–cm) baking sheet with parchment paper or a silicone baking mat.

Using a mortar and pestle or a food processor, grind the dried lavender with the granulated sugar until it's finely textured.

In the bowl of a stand mixer fitted with the paddle attachment, mix the lavender sugar with the brown sugar and butter. Mix on medium until light and fluffy, about 2 to 3 minutes. Add the flour and mix on medium until completely incorporated and the dough begins forming a ball. Remove from the bowl and form into a disk with your hands. Roll out on a lightly floured surface until it is ¼ inch (6 mm) thick. Use a round 2½-inch (6-cm) cookie cutter to cut out cookies, or simply use a knife to cut into squares. If the dough is too sticky to roll out, the butter may have gotten a bit too warm. Simply chill for 15 minutes and try again. Transfer the cookies to the lined baking sheet, gather the scraps and re-roll to cut out more cookies. Sprinkle the tops of the cookies with a bit of coarse sugar for a little extra something, if desired.

Bake for 15 to 17 minutes, or until the edges are lightly browned. Unlike most cookies, I find it better to slightly overbake shortbread rather than under-bake it to ensure you get that melt-in-your-mouth texture. Allow to cool for 5 minutes before transferring to a cooling rack. Serve immediately or store in an airtight container. Shortbread will last about a week at room temperature, but I recommend freezing it right away to keep it at its freshest. It will last about 3 months in the freezer. Simply thaw and serve.

lavender-lemon loaf

Lavender is easy to grow in containers, and it is so fun to dry your own, but if you have the chance to visit a lavender farm, you should! Rows and rows of beautifully scented purple flowers everywhere. And the smell! Truly an amazing experience. The soft, floral flavor of lavender pairs perfectly with the bright, tart zest of lemons. I find the citrus keeps the lavender in check, so there's no soapy taste in sight. This recipe makes two loaves, one to keep and one to gift. Or, you know, . . . one to pop in your freezer for a rainy day— just remember to slice it before you do.

Yield: 2 (5 x 9–inch [13 x 23–cm]) loaves

LOAVES

1 cup (240 ml) whole milk

2½ tbsp (13 g) dried culinary-grade lavender

1½ cups (300 g) granulated sugar

2 tbsp (12 g) lemon zest (about 2 lemons)

1 cup (227 g) butter, room temperature

2 tbsp (30 ml) fresh lemon juice (about 1 lemon)

4 large eggs

3 cups (375 g) all-purpose flour

2 tsp (9 g) baking powder

1 tsp salt

Preheat the oven to 350°F (180°C). Grease two 5 x 9–inch (13 x 23–cm) loaf pans and set aside. (Alternately, you could use two 4 x 8–inch [10 x 20–cm] pans if you'd prefer taller loaves and adjust the baking time as needed.)

To make the loaves, in a small saucepan, stir together the milk and lavender. Heat on medium-low until the mixture starts to steam, but don't let it boil. Turn the heat off, but leave the pan on the burner and let the lavender steep for 5 to 10 minutes. Strain out the lavender with a fine-mesh sieve, and allow the milk to cool slightly. In a medium bowl, stir together the granulated sugar and lemon zest. I like to massage the zest in with my hands, but you can simply use a spatula if you like. Mix until fragrant. In the bowl of a stand mixer fitted with the paddle attachment, add the lemon sugar and butter. Mix on high for 3 to 4 minutes, until pale and fluffy. Add the lemon juice and mix until combined. Add the eggs one at a time, on medium speed, until the batter is smooth.

In a separate bowl, whisk together the flour, baking powder and salt. With the mixer on low, slowly stream half of the lavender milk into the butter-sugar mixture. Then add half of the flour mixture. Repeat with the rest of the milk and then the flour. Mix the batter until just barely combined. Use a spatula to scrape down the sides and bottom of the bowl. Divide the batter between the two prepared pans, gently smooth out the batter with a knife or offset spatula so the tops are flat and bake for 40 to 50 minutes, or until the top of the loaf gently springs back when pressed. Baking time can vary quite a bit depending on the thickness and darkness of your pans, so start checking for doneness at the 40-minute mark. Remove from the oven and allow to cool for 5 to 10 minutes before carefully removing the loaves from the pans and cooling the rest of the way on a cooling rack.

While the loaves are baking, prepare the lemon simple syrup and/or the lemon glaze. I usually choose to do either the syrup or the glaze, but you're welcome to do both if you'd like!

(continued)

LEMON SIMPLE SYRUP

2 tbsp (30 ml) fresh lemon juice (about 1 lemon)

2–3 tbsp (30–45 g) granulated sugar, or to taste

LEMON GLAZE

2 tbsp (30 ml) fresh lemon juice (about 1 lemon)

3 tbsp (45 ml) melted unsalted butter

1 cup (120 g) powdered sugar, plus more as needed

Milk or cream, if needed to adjust consistency

To make the simple syrup, in a small bowl, stir together the lemon juice with the sugar until dissolved. Generously brush the loaves while they're still hot from the oven for a lovely punch of flavor.

For the lemon glaze, in a medium bowl, mix the lemon juice, melted butter and powdered sugar until smooth. Adjust the consistency with more powdered sugar or a splash of milk. Pour the glaze over cooled loaves, otherwise it may run off.

This loaf is best served on the first day, but it will keep for several days in an airtight container at room temperature. The loaf also freezes well. Slice the loaf first and then place in an airtight container. When ready to serve, remove from the freezer and allow to come to room temperature, or warm slightly in the oven, if desired.

Seasonal Substitutes

Swap the dried lavender for other dried flowers such as rose or even fresh rosemary. Adjust to taste when steeping.

fresh mint nanaimo bars

Nanaimo bars are a Canadian dessert made up of three layers: a coconut crumb base, a creamy custard filling and a chocolate top! Striking when cut, but easy to assemble. I put my own spin on this classic by adding fresh mint leaves to the custard layer and swapping in chocolate crumbs instead of graham cracker crumbs for the base. As always, you can customize the strength of the flavor to your own personal preference. Nanaimo bars are decadent and are best served in small pieces.

Yield: 1 (8 x 8–inch [20 x 20–cm]) pan, about 16 servings

BASE LAYER

1 tbsp (8 g) ground flaxseed

3 tbsp (45 ml) water

⅓ cup (80 ml) melted unsalted butter

1½ cups (150 g) chocolate baking crumbs, such as Oreo Baking Crumbs

1 cup (93 g) shredded unsweetened coconut

2 tbsp (30 g) granulated sugar

½ tsp vanilla extract

⅛ tsp salt

CUSTARD LAYER

1½ tbsp (5 g) finely chopped fresh mint leaves (can substitute with mint extract to taste)

¼ cup (57 g) unsalted butter, softened

3 tbsp (45 ml) whole milk

2 tbsp (20 g) custard powder

2 cups (240 g) powdered sugar

CHOCOLATE LAYER

1 cup (175 g) semisweet chocolate chips or chopped chocolate

1½ tbsp (21 g) vegetable shortening

Line an 8 x 8–inch (20 x 20–cm) pan with parchment paper, making sure the parchment reaches the top of each side of the pan so it can be easily lifted out and the bars can be cut once assembled.

To make the base layer, in a small bowl, stir together the ground flaxseed and water. Set aside. In a separate bowl, stir together the melted butter, chocolate baking crumbs, shredded coconut, sugar, vanilla extract and salt. Stir in the flaxseed mixture until well combined. Firmly press the crumb mixture into the prepared pan and place in the fridge to set while you prepare the next layer.

To make the custard layer, muddle the mint leaves using a mortar and pestle, the bottom of a cup or the end of a wooden spoon. This will help release the leaves' flavor. Place in a medium bowl with the softened butter, milk, custard powder and powdered sugar. Mix on medium until smooth. Test and adjust the strength of the mint if necessary. I find the flavor tends to mellow out the more the bars sit, so start with a stronger flavor than you might think. Spread the custard layer over the chilled crumb layer and place back into the fridge.

To make the chocolate layer, in a medium saucepan, melt the chocolate and shortening together on medium-low heat, stirring constantly, until smooth. The shortening is vital in helping the chocolate layer from becoming completely solid, which would crack when cutting and eating. Remove from the heat and allow to cool for about 5 minutes before spreading smoothly over the custard layer.

Place the assembled bars back into the fridge for about 5 minutes, or until the chocolate has begun to set but is not hard. Remove from the fridge and lightly score the chocolate layer with a sharp knife. This scoring process will help them not crack once you cut them when they're fully chilled. Return the pan to the fridge for at least 30 minutes. Use the parchment paper to lift the bars out of the pan and carefully cut all the squares. Serve or store in an airtight container in the fridge for up to a week.

for the love of berries

Summer arrives with berries upon berries. My hometown, Abbotsford, British Columbia, is known as the berry capital of Canada, which means that we're pretty spoiled when it comes to our berry selection. Rows and rows of blueberries and raspberries are a common sight, and woe to the poor fellow who gets stuck behind a slow-moving berry machine. On a hot afternoon, the smell of raspberries, in particular, lingers heavily in the air and is one of the better smells that a farm can share with the neighborhood . . . if you know what I mean.

Hot and sticky summer days were spent in the berry patch for much of my childhood. For many years, our farm grew raspberries, blackberries, blueberries and saskatoons until our fall market grew too big for us to keep up with everything. Rainbow-stained hands were a given. All our berry crops were picked by hand, which meant many long days, evenings and weekends in the berry patch as a family, making sure all of our orders were met and that no berries went to waste. Berries slow down their ripening speed for no one and need to be continuously harvested, no matter what. While it was simply work back then, as an adult, I find myself hunting down local farms so I can pick my own berries again. It truly is a lovely experience to pick your own food, spend some quiet time in a berry patch and support a local farmer! You'll usually save a bit of money this way too, which is a win-win.

I find berries to be so special with all the ways you can use them. Eat them fresh; use them as a topping; make them into sauces, jams or compotes; or bake with them! They're fairly easy to swap for one another, so feel free to experiment with whatever you have on hand.

From a crowd-pleasing Chocolate-Zucchini Sheet Cake with Strawberry Swiss Meringue Frosting (page 51) (a cheeky nod at zucchinis being part of the berry family!) to an eye-catching Blackberry-Lime No-Bake Cheesecake (page 73), their flavors are elevated when matched with simple favorites. Pair blueberries' sweet juiciness with the tart punch of lemon curd in a fun twist on a classic muffin (page 52), or fold saskatoons, which are slightly smaller and nuttier than blueberries, into a cloud-like angel food cake (page 77). Despite the heat of the summer months, they truly are some of the most abundant and inspiring weeks to bake in.

bumbleberry braided lattice pie with rye crust

A bumbleberry pie is another Canadian dessert! It simply refers to a mixed berry pie and often contains rhubarb and/or apples as well. Pretty much all my favorite things! Feel free to mix in whatever berries you prefer or happen to have on hand. I like to have a good balance of sweet and tart flavors going on, and throwing in some rhubarb or apples helps give the pie some great structure.

Yield: 1 (9-inch [23-cm]) pie

PIE

1 cup (200 g) granulated sugar

½ cup (63 g) all-purpose flour

1 tsp ground cinnamon

1½ cups (222 g) blueberries

1¼ cups (180 g) blackberries

1¼ cups (190 g) halved strawberries

2 cups (202 g) chopped rhubarb (½" [1.3-cm] pieces) or cubed tart apple

1 batch Pie Dough with rye flour variation (page 191), divided into two disks

1 cup (123 g) raspberries

CRUST TOPPING

1 large egg

1 tbsp (15 ml) cream or milk

Coarse sugar, as needed

> *Note:* The pie crust will need to be prepared at least 1 hour before starting the pie, but preferably the day before. Pie crust will keep in an airtight container in the fridge for 2 to 3 days, or for up to 3 months in the freezer. (Thaw in the fridge before using.)

In a small bowl, whisk together the sugar, flour and cinnamon. Set aside. In a large bowl, mix the blueberries, blackberries, strawberries and rhubarb with a wooden spoon. Sprinkle the prepared sugar-flour mixture on top and stir together until distributed evenly. Set aside. (Keep the raspberries separate, as they'll simply get squished into jam if mixed with the rest of the filling.)

Remove one pie dough disk from the fridge for the bottom pie crust, and on a lightly floured surface, roll it out in a circle about ⅛ inch (3 mm) thick. Depending on how long the dough has chilled and the temperature of your house, it may need to hang out on the counter for 10 to 20 minutes to warm up a little so it doesn't crack as you roll it out. The circle should be 2 to 3 inches (5 to 8 cm) wider than your pie dish on all sides. Carefully transfer the dough into a 9-inch (23-cm) diameter pie dish and trim the edges so that about 1 inch (2.5 cm) hangs past the edge of the dish. Place the filling into the pie dish and sprinkle the raspberries on top. Transfer to the fridge to keep the bottom crust chilled while you prepare the top crust. Repeat the above steps for a simple double crust, or follow the steps found on page 192 for a lattice top.

Preheat the oven to 425°F (220°C) while the pie is chilling in the freezer.

To make the crust topping, in a small bowl, use a fork to lightly beat the egg and mix in the cream. Remove the pie from the freezer and brush the entire crust with the egg wash (try and get under the lattice a bit too), working quickly. Sprinkle with coarse sugar and immediately place in the oven.

Bake for 15 minutes and then reduce the temperature to 350°F (180°C). Bake for 40 to 50 minutes, or until the crust is golden and the filling is bubbling. Check on the pie a few times as it's baking, and cover the crust with a pie shield or a bit of aluminum foil if it is browning too much. Remove from the oven and allow to cool on a cooling rack for at least 1 to 2 hours before cutting. If you cut it while it's still quite warm, the filling will be runny, as it hasn't had a chance to set. This is best served with ice cream. Keep loosely covered for 1 to 2 days or a couple days longer in the fridge.

chocolate-zucchini sheet cake
with strawberry swiss meringue frosting

Did you know that from a purely botanical perspective zucchinis are technically a berry? And that straw-berries aren't? Things get tricky in the fruit world. I should know, as I studied ecology at university! The years after high school were spent away from the farm while I got my degree, although summers were still spent working alongside my family. Zucchinis seem like a good idea to plant at the beginning of the season, and then suddenly you have a mountain of them at your feet, and none of the neighbors will accept them anymore. Ha! Cake made with zucchini is both deliciously moist and technically has some fruit in it!

Yield: 1 (9 x 13–inch [23 x 33–cm]) cake

CAKE

3 cups (375 g) all-purpose flour

2 cups (400 g) granulated sugar

2 tsp (9 g) baking soda

½ tsp salt

⅔ cup (57 g) cocoa powder

2 tbsp (30 ml) white vinegar

¾ cup (180 ml) vegetable oil

1 tbsp (15 ml) vanilla extract

½ cup (120 ml) water

1½ cups (186 g) grated zucchini

STRAWBERRY FROSTING

1 cup (152 g) halved strawberries

1 cup (227 g) unsalted butter, room temperature

1 tsp vanilla extract

3 cups (360 g) powdered sugar, divided

Milk or cream, if needed to adjust consistency

FOR SERVING

Halved strawberries, for decorating

Sprinkles (optional)

Preheat the oven to 350°F (180°C). Grease a 9 x 13–inch (23 x 33–cm) pan if you'll be serving the cake right in the pan or line with parchment paper for easier removal of the cake. Set aside.

To make the cake, in a large bowl, whisk together the flour, sugar, baking soda, salt and cocoa powder until completely combined. Add the vinegar, oil, vanilla and water and stir together with a spatula. Mix in the grated zucchini. Pour the batter into the prepared pan and bake for 30 to 35 minutes, or until a toothpick comes out clean. If serving the cake right from the pan, simply cool in the pan on a cooling rack. Alternatively, use the parchment paper to lift the cake out of the pan after it's cooled for 5 to 10 minutes.

To make the frosting, preheat the oven to 350°F (180°C). Place the halved strawberries in a single layer in a glass 8 x 8–inch (20 x 20–cm) baking dish. Bake for 15 to 20 minutes, or until the berries are soft and juicing. Allow to cool for a few minutes and then puree in a blender until smooth. Place the strawberry puree into a small saucepan and simmer on medium heat, stirring constantly, until the sauce thickens slightly, about 5 minutes. Allow to cool completely. The sauce will thicken further as it cools.

In the bowl of a stand mixer fitted with the whisk attachment, add the butter and mix on medium-high for 3 to 5 minutes, or until the butter is smooth and has lightened in color. Switch to the paddle attachment. Add the vanilla extract and 2 cups (240 g) of the powdered sugar. Mix on medium-low until well combined. Add the cooled strawberry puree, mix on low until combined and then add the remaining powdered sugar. Mix on medium-low until the frosting is nice and smooth. It should be soft enough to spread but stiff enough to hold its shape. Adjust the consistency by adding more powdered sugar or a splash of milk if necessary. Make sure the cake is completely cool before frosting. Frost the cake and top with halved strawberries or sprinkles, if desired. Store in an airtight container at room temperature for several days. It freezes very well.

blueberry–lemon curd muffins

My sister Jordyn was our farm's fastest berry picker. She could out-pick anyone, and her favorite berry to pick was blueberries. Jordyn and I often came up with interesting projects in the kitchen when we were together, and of course berries were a common ingredient. These muffins put a spin on a classic by adding a dollop of lemon curd to each muffin before it is baked. The curd adds a great creamy texture to the muffins, and the crumb topping is a must.

Yield: 12 muffins

CRUMB TOPPING

¼ cup (55 g) packed brown sugar

2 tbsp (30 g) granulated sugar

⅔ cup (83 g) all-purpose flour

1 tsp ground cinnamon

¼ cup (60 ml) melted butter

Pinch of salt

MUFFINS

½ cup (110 g) packed brown sugar

¼ cup (50 g) granulated sugar

½ cup (114 g) unsalted butter, softened

2 large eggs

¾ cup (180 ml) plain Greek yogurt

2 tsp (10 ml) vanilla extract

2 cups (250 g) all-purpose flour

1 tbsp (14 g) baking powder

¾ tsp salt

1 cup (148 g) fresh or frozen blueberries

1 cup (240 ml) Lemon Curd (page 208)

Preheat the oven to 400°F (200°C). Grease two muffin tins and set aside.

To make the crumb topping, in a medium bowl, stir together the brown sugar, granulated sugar, flour, cinnamon, melted butter and salt with your hands. The mixture will form crumbs as you squeeze it in your hand, and you can control the size of the chunks. Place the mixture in the fridge until ready to use.

To make the muffins, in the bowl of a stand mixer fitted with the paddle attachment, cream together the brown sugar, granulated sugar and softened butter on high for 2 to 3 minutes, or until light and fluffy. Beat in the eggs on medium-low speed, one at a time, until well mixed. Mix in the yogurt and vanilla extract on low, scraping down the sides with a spatula as you go. Set aside. In a medium bowl, whisk together the flour, baking powder and salt. Gradually add this to the wet mixture, mixing on low, until mostly incorporated with a few streaks of flour remaining. Use a spatula to scrape down the sides, and then gently fold in the blueberries until the batter has just come together. The batter will be very thick; that's just right.

Spoon the batter into the prepared muffin tins. I like to use an ice cream scoop to make this nice and easy. I usually skip every other muffin spot to get even higher muffin tops! So, it will go: batter, no batter, batter. And then the next line will be: no batter, batter, no batter. Not strictly necessary, but it does help the muffins get a better rise. Use the back of a spoon to create a small dip in the center of each muffin, and spoon about 1 tablespoon (15 ml) of lemon curd into the dip. Add the crumbs on top of everything, dividing evenly between the 12 muffins. Bake for 5 minutes. Reduce the temperature to 350°F (180°C) and bake for 12 to 15 minutes, or until an inserted toothpick comes out clean or with just a few moist crumbs. (But do your best to avoid poking a toothpick into the curd.) Remove the muffins, place them on a cooling rack and allow them to cool for 5 to 10 minutes before removing from their pan. Serve warm. As with most muffins, these are best on the first day; otherwise, let them cool completely and move to an airtight container in the fridge for a couple of days or to the freezer for a couple of months.

Seasonal Substitutes

Use cranberries, rhubarb, apples or peaches in place of the blueberries. Lime or grapefruit curd are also fun variations.

blueberry–earl grey cream roll cake

Blueberries grow on bushes that are just the right height to either stand or sit on a bucket to pick, without having to reach too high. Many warm, summer evenings were spent with friends and family picking blueberries for fresh orders. One memorable night, before the days of iPhones and portable speakers, we turned the radio on in one of the cars for some music, only to realize a couple hours later that it had come at the cost of the battery. We then had to jump-start the car to get it out of the field, but it was worth it! That time spent with friends was so special to us, as they rallied around us during a high-stress season. We would often end the night gathering on the patio with dessert, and it taught me from an early age that not only does food bring people together, but that it has been my family's way of saying "thank you" to so many of those around us. Cake is a great thing to serve at these kinds of gatherings, and this easier-than-it-looks jelly roll is no exception. Pillowy white cake infused with earl grey tea is rolled up around pale purple blueberry whipped cream, creating a striking visual that is sure to impress your friends. Make sure the cake is well chilled to ensure the cleanest cuts!

Yield: 1 jelly roll cake

CAKE

⅓ cup (80 ml) whole milk, plus more as needed

3 tbsp (6 g) loose-leaf earl grey tea

4 large eggs

1 cup (200 g) granulated sugar

½ tsp vanilla extract

1 cup (125 g) all-purpose flour

1 tsp baking powder

¼ tsp salt

Preheat the oven to 375°F (190°C). Line a 10 x 15–inch (25 x 38–cm) rimmed jelly roll pan with parchment paper. The parchment paper should hang over each edge about ½ inch (1.3 cm). Set aside.

To make the cake, in a small saucepan, heat the milk on medium until steaming. Remove from the heat, add the earl grey tea and steep for 3 minutes. Pour the milk through a strainer to remove the tea leaves, making sure to press them firmly to squeeze out all the milk. Remeasure the milk and top off if needed to get back to ⅓ cup (80 ml). Let it cool slightly before using. In the bowl of a stand mixer fitted with the paddle attachment, mix the eggs, sugar and vanilla on medium speed. Reduce to medium-low and slowly stream in the milk mixture. Increase the speed to high for 1 minute, or until the batter is well mixed. In a medium bowl, whisk together the flour, baking powder and salt. Add to the wet ingredients, and mix on low until just combined. Use a spatula to scrape down the sides and bottom of the bowl. Pour the batter into the prepared pan and spread into a thin, even layer.

Bake for 10 to 12 minutes, or until the top is lightly golden and the cake springs back when gently poked. It's important that your oven is level, otherwise you'll get an uneven cake! Remove from the oven and carefully remove the cake from the hot pan. Roll it up short end to short end, with the parchment paper in between the layers so the cake doesn't stick to itself. The cake will be hot, so you may need to wear oven mitts during this process. Cool for 1 to 2 hours before filling, otherwise the cake will melt the whipped cream.

(continued)

BLUEBERRY WHIPPED CREAM

1 cup (148 g) fresh or frozen blueberries

2 tbsp (30 ml) water

1 tbsp (15 g) granulated sugar

1½ cups (360 ml) whipping cream

1 tbsp (8 g) powdered sugar

FOR SERVING

Fresh blueberries (optional)

Fresh thyme or mint (optional)

To make the whipped cream, in a small saucepan, heat the blueberries, water and granulated sugar until the berries start to break down. Simmer for about 10 minutes, or until the mixture starts getting thick and jammy. Remove from the heat and cool. Chill in the fridge before using. In the bowl of a stand mixer fitted with the whisk attachment, whip the whipping cream on high for 2 to 4 minutes, or until medium peaks form. Add the powdered sugar and continue mixing until stiff peaks form. Use a spatula to gently fold in the chilled blueberry mixture, working carefully so the whipped cream doesn't deflate. This mixture does not have to be perfectly mixed as the swirls of purple are lovely. Reserve about 1 cup (240 ml) to pipe on top of the cake before serving.

To assemble, carefully unroll the cooled cake and remove the parchment paper. The cake will want to stay rolled up and may crack slightly. That's normal! Spread a generous layer of blueberry whipped cream on the cake, leaving about a ½-inch (1.3-cm) border on the outside edges where the cream may push out. Carefully roll the cake back up as tight as you can and chill in an airtight container in the fridge until ready to serve. Top with the reserved whipped cream, fresh blueberries and fresh thyme or mint, if desired.

Seasonal Substitutes

Fold in 1 cup (240 ml) of Lemon Curd (page 208) instead of the berry mixture for an excellent winter treat. Frozen blueberries also work great in this recipe out of season. Find tips for freezing fruit on page 210.

blueberry-basil tart with shortbread crust

Growing up with a near-endless supply of blueberries was one of the biggest perks of life on the farm. It meant a lot of experimentation occurred of course! I loved combining different herbs and spices to see how they complemented—or clashed with—the sweet, juicy blueberries. To date, one of the best combinations has been blueberry and basil. This bright-hued tart combines these flavors in the filling and is easily adjusted to taste.

Yield: 1 (10-inch [25-cm]) tart

SHORTBREAD CRUST

½ cup (114 g) unsalted butter, softened

1½ cups (188 g) all-purpose flour

⅓ cup (40 g) powdered sugar

⅛ tsp salt

Milk, as needed

BLUEBERRY COMPOTE

2½ cups (370 g) fresh or frozen blueberries

2 tbsp (30 ml) water

1 tbsp (15 g) granulated sugar

BLUEBERRY-BASIL FILLING

Blueberry compote (see above)

¼ cup (60 ml) fresh lemon juice (about 2 lemons)

1 tbsp (8 g) cornstarch

⅔ cup (132 g) granulated sugar

5 large egg yolks

1 tsp vanilla extract

2 tbsp (5 g) minced fresh basil leaves, plus more to taste

¼ cup (57 g) unsalted butter, softened

FOR SERVING

Fresh blueberries (optional)

Fresh basil leaves (optional)

Whipped cream (optional)

Chocolate curls (optional)

Preheat the oven to 350°F (180°C).

To make the crust, in the bowl of a stand mixer fitted with the paddle attachment, mix the softened butter, flour, powdered sugar and salt on medium until it starts to form coarse crumbs, about 1 to 2 minutes. Squeeze a few crumbs together in the palm of your hand—they should stick together. If the dough seems too crumbly, add a tablespoon (15 ml) or more of milk. Press the crumbs firmly into the bottom of a 10-inch (25-cm) round tart pan (with removable bottom, if possible). Bake for 12 to 15 minutes, or until golden brown. Set aside to cool.

To make the blueberry compote, place the blueberries, water and sugar into a medium saucepan and cook on medium heat, mashing the berries down with a wooden spoon as they start to soften. Once the berries have broken down, about 5 minutes, remove from the heat and allow to cool slightly. Blend smooth using a high-speed blender or immersion blender and strain if desired.

To make the filling, place the prepared blueberry compote into a clean, medium saucepan. In a small bowl, mix the lemon juice and cornstarch until it is completely smooth. Don't add cornstarch directly to the berries, or to any warm mixture, as you will get lumps. Add the cornstarch mixture to the blueberry compote and stir in the granulated sugar and egg yolks. Heat the mixture over medium heat, stirring constantly, until the temperature reaches 165°F (74°C) and the mixture is thick and jammy.

Remove from the heat, then whisk in the vanilla extract, minced basil and butter, 1 tablespoon (15 g) at a time. Mix until completely smooth. Taste the filling at this point and add more basil, if desired. Pour the filling into the tart shell and let cool to room temperature before transferring to the fridge in an airtight container. Chill completely before serving, at least 4 hours or overnight. Immediately before serving, top with fresh blueberries, basil leaves, whipped cream or whatever your heart desires. Chocolate would be a wonderful addition as well. This tart will keep for several days in the fridge in an airtight container.

gluten-free raspberry brownies

I was lucky that growing up on the farm meant that my parents were around a lot. They worked from home and their schedules could often be quite flexible. This, of course, was balanced with hectic harvest times where more sacrifices had to be made, as it was hard for them to leave their work at work. My mom loved to bake and passed that on to my sister and me. She gave us the freedom and confidence to make a mess in the kitchen, as long as we cleaned up after ourselves. From a young age we started baking on our own, with the knowledge that she was always in earshot if things went sideways. Brownies were one of the first recipes I mastered. Mix all the batter in a bowl and bake. Nice and easy. This version features coconut flour, which happens to make it gluten free but also adds a wonderful texture and subtle flavor. Raspberries are stirred in and sprinkled on top at the end and add a wonderful zing to these rich bars.

Yield: 1 (9 x 13–inch [23 x 33–cm]) pan

1 cup (240 ml) melted unsalted butter

3 cups (600 g) granulated sugar

1 tbsp (15 ml) vanilla extract

4 large eggs

¾ cup (84 g) coconut flour

1 cup (88 g) unsweetened cocoa powder

1 tsp salt

1 cup (123 g) fresh or frozen raspberries (do not thaw if using frozen berries)

Powdered sugar, to taste (optional)

Preheat the oven to 350°F (180°C). Grease a 9 x 13–inch (23 x 33–cm) baking dish or line with parchment paper for easier removal from the pan. Set aside.

In the bowl of a stand mixer fitted with the paddle attachment, cream the butter, sugar and vanilla extract for 2 to 3 minutes on medium-high. Beat in the eggs one at a time, mixing on medium until fully incorporated. Scrape down the sides and bottom of the bowl with a spatula between each addition. In a separate bowl, sift together the coconut flour, cocoa powder and salt. Gradually add the flour mixture to the butter mixture, mixing on low speed. Mix until just moist and no flour traces are left. Gently fold half of the raspberries into the batter. Be sure to use a spatula to scrape down the sides and bottom of the bowl. Scrape batter into the prepared pan and sprinkle the remaining raspberries evenly over the top.

Bake for 35 to 40 minutes, or until a toothpick inserted into the center comes out with just a few moist crumbs. Remove from the oven and allow to cool slightly before cutting and serving. Sprinkle with powdered sugar directly before serving, if desired. These are best served warm (and with ice cream). Store in the fridge for up to 4 days.

raspberry-almond cake

It wasn't unusual for my family to spend weekends in the raspberry fields when I was growing up, doing our best to keep up with berries that would wait for nobody. Overripe berries equal mushy messes and make picking tougher than it should be. Sometimes our grandma would join my sister and me, and it was always a highlight. She had grown up picking berries with her sisters, and they were all speedsters. Grandma was an incredibly hard worker and would often sneak her own berry baskets into our flats, letting us earn a little extra cash, which made working weekends not quite so bad. Raspberries will always remind me of her, although I no longer have to pick them for work. Two of her favorite things were traveling and baking, and I love that I share that with her. I was inspired by a raspberry cake I tried in Edinburgh, and I knew I had to put my own spin on it. Homemade almond paste is the star of the show (store-bought works fine, too) and gives this cake the most wonderful texture. It's quick and simple to make, I promise! Almonds and raspberries are heaven together, as the nutty flavor grounds the tartness deliciously well.

Yield: 1 (9-inch [23-cm]) round cake

HOMEMADE ALMOND PASTE
(yields 2 cups [454 g])

2½ cups (240 g) almond flour, plus extra if needed

1½ cups (180 g) powdered sugar, plus extra if needed

Pinch of salt

1 large egg white

¼ tsp almond extract

Cold water, if needed

Note: You can substitute 1½ cups (215 g) of whole, blanched almonds in place of almond flour and use a food processor to grind into a fine flour.

To make the almond paste, combine the almond flour, sugar and a pinch of salt in a food processor. Mix briefly until combined. Add the egg white and almond extract and process until a smooth paste forms. Alternatively, simply mix all ingredients with a hand mixer until the paste starts to come together. The mixture may look quite crumbly at first, as if it won't come together. Squeeze some of the paste in your hand to see if it will hold. If it doesn't, add a couple teaspoons of water to the mixture and mix together.

Turn the almond paste out onto a surface lightly dusted with powdered sugar and knead the paste together with your hands. Again, if the paste seems too crumbly, add a few teaspoons of cold water. If the paste seems too wet and is too sticky to work with, add a few tablespoons of almond flour or powdered sugar until smooth. The paste can be used immediately, or divide it in half and form each half into a log. Wrap tightly in plastic wrap and place into an airtight container in the fridge or freezer. The paste will last about 3 months in the fridge or 6 months in the freezer. Let the paste come to room temperature before using in a recipe.

Preheat the oven to 350°F (180°C). Grease a 9-inch (23-cm) springform cake pan, or use a 9-inch (23-cm) pan lined with parchment paper for easy removal. Set aside.

(continued)

CAKE

1 cup (200 g) granulated sugar

1 cup (227 g) store-bought or homemade almond paste (see page 62)

¾ cup (170 g) unsalted butter, room temperature

½ tsp vanilla extract

½ tsp almond extract

4 large eggs

1½ cups (188 g) all-purpose flour

1½ tsp (7 g) baking powder

¼ tsp salt

2 cups (246 g) fresh or frozen raspberries, divided

⅓ cup (36 g) slivered almonds

Powdered sugar (optional)

To make the cake, in the bowl of a stand mixer fitted with the paddle attachment, mix the granulated sugar with the almond paste on low for 3 to 5 minutes, until completely combined. The mixture should look sandy. Add the butter and vanilla and almond extracts and increase mixer speed to medium-high. Mix for 2 minutes until well combined and fluffy. Reduce the speed to medium-low and add the eggs one at a time, mixing until mostly combined after each one. The batter may look curdled during this process, but don't worry! It will come together as we add the flour. In a small bowl, whisk together the flour, baking powder and salt. Slowly add to the wet ingredients and mix on low until just combined, trying not to overmix. Use a spatula to scrape down the sides and bottom of the bowl. Carefully fold in 1½ cups (185 g) of the raspberries. Scrape the batter into the prepared pan, and top with the remaining raspberries and slivered almonds.

Bake for 50 to 60 minutes, or until the center has set. Remove the cake from the oven, place it onto a cooling rack and run a sharp knife along the edges to help loosen it from the pan. Allow to cool almost completely in the springform pan, remove and serve. Dust with powdered sugar directly before serving, if desired. Store in an airtight container in the fridge for up to 4 days. Slice and freeze for up to 3 months; allow to come to room temperature before serving, and warm slightly in the oven, if desired.

Seasonal Substitutes

Blueberries, blackberries or diced apples can be subbed in place of the raspberries. Frozen berries work nicely as they don't lose their shape when mixed into the dense batter.

raspberry tart with chocolate crust and ganache

Summers as a kid went like this: Wake up, go pick berries until lunchtime, then our time was ours again—free to swim or rollerblade. This routine instilled the value of hard work balanced with play. Work hard, play hard. This raspberry tart involves a few more steps than some of the simpler recipes in this book, but it's worth it. Use a tart pan with a removable bottom or simply make it in a shallow pie dish.

Yield: 1 (9-inch [23-cm]) round tart

CRUST

1½ cups (150 g) chocolate baking crumbs, such as Oreo Baking Crumbs

¼ cup (50 g) granulated sugar

6 tbsp (90 ml) melted unsalted butter

RASPBERRY SAUCE

2 cups (246 g) raspberries

1 tsp lemon juice

4 tbsp (60 ml) cold water, divided

½ tbsp (4 g) cornstarch

½ tsp vanilla extract

FILLING

¾ cup (180 ml) raspberry sauce (see above)

½ cup (116 g) plain cream cheese, at room temperature

2 tbsp (16 g) powdered sugar

¼ cup (60 ml) plain skyr yogurt or thick Greek yogurt

CHOCOLATE GANACHE

¼ cup (60 ml) whipping cream

1 cup (150 g) chopped bittersweet or semisweet chocolate

2 tbsp (28 g) unsalted butter

½ tsp vanilla extract

FOR SERVING

Fresh raspberries (optional)

Chopped pistachios (optional)

Preheat the oven to 350°F (180°C).

To make the crust, in a small bowl, stir together the chocolate baking crumbs, sugar and melted butter. Press firmly into the bottom and up the sides of a 9-inch (23-cm) tart pan with removable bottom or shallow pie dish. The edges should be about ¼ inch (6 mm) thick. Bake the crust for 8 to 10 minutes, or until fragrant. Remove from the oven and set aside to cool as you mix together the filling.

To make the raspberry sauce, in a medium saucepan, add the raspberries, lemon juice and 2 tablespoons (30 ml) of water and cook on medium heat. Mash the raspberries down as they start to cook and bring to a gentle simmer. In a small bowl, mix the remaining 2 tablespoons (30 ml) of water and cornstarch together until smooth. If the cornstarch is mixed into warm water or straight into the sauce, it won't dissolve well and will likely be lumpy. Stream into the raspberry sauce and cook for 1 to 2 minutes, or until the sauce has thickened. Remove from the heat, strain through a fine-mesh sieve, stir in the vanilla extract and set aside to cool. This should yield about ¾ cup (180 ml) of sauce, although the exact amount may differ slightly depending on cook time and seed volume.

Once the raspberry sauce has cooled to room temperature, prepare the filling. In the bowl of a stand mixer fitted with the paddle attachment, combine ¾ cup (180 ml) of the cooled raspberry sauce, cream cheese, powdered sugar and skyr yogurt. Mix on low until the mixture is completely smooth. Pour over the cooled chocolate crust and place in the fridge while you prepare the ganache.

To make the chocolate ganache, in a small saucepan, heat the whipping cream on medium until it comes to a gentle simmer. Immediately shut off the heat and add the chopped chocolate, butter and vanilla extract. Don't stir yet! Remove from the heat and let sit undisturbed for 3 minutes. Then start whisking the mixture until a smooth, shiny ganache forms. If the chocolate pieces aren't quite melted, simply place back on the burner on low heat until everything is smooth. Pour over the chilled raspberry filling and use an offset spatula to smooth the ganache into an even layer.

Place the tart in the fridge and allow to set for at least an hour before serving. Garnish with fresh raspberries and chopped pistachios, if desired. Store leftover tart in an airtight container in the fridge for 2 to 3 days.

blackberry-filled vanilla cupcakes with white chocolate frosting

Picking blackberries was always a slightly treacherous affair. Ours were unfortunately not the thornless variety, and no matter how cautious you were, your arms were bound to bear rows of scratches in no time. This did little to dissuade our enthusiasm for picking them though, as they weigh more than any other berry and added up quickly. They also didn't squish easily. That's a win-win on a hot summer's day. These cupcakes combine the tart punch of flavor of blackberries with fluffy white cake, and are topped with a rich white chocolate buttercream. Don't be shy about filling them with blackberry compote, as it really is the star of the show and helps keep the sweetness of this dessert in check. Keep the cupcakes in the fridge once piped and the frosting sets nice and firm, which makes them easily transportable!

Yield: 20–24 cupcakes

CUPCAKES

4 egg whites

1 tsp vanilla extract

1 tsp almond extract

¾ cup (180 ml) whole milk, divided

2⅓ cups (280 g) cake flour

2 tsp (9 g) baking powder

¼ tsp salt

1 cup (200 g) granulated sugar

¾ cup (170 g) unsalted butter, softened

BLACKBERRY COMPOTE

2 cups (288 g) fresh or frozen blackberries

1 tbsp (15 g) granulated sugar

1 tbsp (15 ml) water

1 tsp cornstarch

Preheat the oven to 350°F (180°C). Line two cupcake tins with cupcake liners and set aside.

To make the cupcakes, in a medium bowl, whisk together the egg whites, vanilla, almond extract and ½ cup (120 ml) of the milk. Set aside. In the bowl of a stand mixer fitted with the paddle attachment, mix together the flour, baking powder, salt and sugar on low. Add the softened butter and remaining milk and mix on low until just moistened. Scrape down the sides and bottom of the bowl. With the mixer on medium-low, slowly stream in the egg white mixture in 3 batches, each one taking about 10 to 15 seconds to add. Ensure everything is completely incorporated before adding the next batch. Once all the ingredients have been added, try not to overmix. Finish mixing with a spatula, carefully folding the batter together and scraping down the sides and bottom of the bowl. Distribute the batter into the two prepared cupcake pans, filling each tin about half to three-quarters full. The exact yield will vary depending on how you fill these. Bake both pans at the same time if possible, for 15 to 16 minutes, or until an inserted toothpick comes out clean. Remove from the oven and cool for 5 minutes before carefully removing the cupcakes from their pans. Allow to cool completely before frosting.

To prepare the blackberry compote, in a medium saucepan, combine the blackberries and sugar over medium heat. In a separate small bowl, stir the water and cornstarch together until smooth and then add to the saucepan. Cook the berries for 5 to 10 minutes, mashing down as they soften. When the berries have broken down and the mixture is thick, remove from the heat and set aside to cool.

(continued)

blackberry-filled vanilla cupcakes with white chocolate frosting (continued)

WHITE CHOCOLATE
BUTTERCREAM

1⅓ cups (200 g) chopped high-quality white chocolate

1 cup (227 g) unsalted butter, softened

2–3 cups (240–360 g) powdered sugar

1 tsp vanilla extract

Pinch of salt

Milk, as needed

FOR SERVING

Sprinkles (optional)

To prepare the white chocolate buttercream, create a double boiler to melt the white chocolate. Simmer a few inches of water in a saucepan over medium-high heat and place a heatproof bowl on top of it but not touching the water. Place the chocolate into the top bowl and stir until the chocolate has melted completely. Set aside to cool to almost room temperature, but not enough for it to resolidify. If it's too warm when added to the rest of the frosting, it will melt the butter and create a soupy mess.

In the bowl of a stand mixer fitted with the paddle attachment, beat the softened butter on medium-high for 2 to 3 minutes, or until pale in color and fluffy. Add 2 cups (240 g) of the powdered sugar and mix together on low. Add the vanilla extract and salt. With the mixer on low, slowly pour in the white chocolate. Use a spatula to scrape down the sides and bottom of the mixing bowl. Continue to mix on medium until the frosting is smooth. You may need to add a splash of milk or a bit more powdered sugar to reach your desired consistency. If the frosting has turned soupy, the chocolate was likely too warm. Simply place it in the fridge for 10 to 15 minutes and try mixing it together again.

To assemble the cupcakes, use a small knife to cut a 1-inch (2.5-cm)-diameter circle out of the top of each cupcake. Angle the knife toward the middle of the cupcake as you cut each circle so that when you pull off the top of the cupcake it should be cone-shaped. Reserve this top as it will go back on the cupcake. Fill the center of the cupcake with about a tablespoon (15 ml) of blackberry compote. Cut the bottom of the reserved cupcake cone off so that just the top circle sits on the blackberry compote without pushing the compote out. Repeat for each cupcake.

For the frosting, place a large star tip into a piping bag and spoon the frosting into the bag. Pipe rosettes by starting in the center of the cupcake and moving in a clockwise circle motion until you reach the outside edge of the cupcake. Alternatively, pipe cupcake swirls or simply frost with a knife. Immediately top with sprinkles, if using, so that they stick to the frosting. Repeat for all the cupcakes. This is best served immediately. Store extras in an airtight container in the fridge for 2 to 3 days, or in the freezer for a couple of months. Thaw in the fridge before serving.

blackberry-lime no-bake cheesecake

There are few things more terrifying than stepping on an underground wasp nest. One minute you're peace-fully picking berries. The next? You're running for your life! Luckily, you shouldn't be chased by any wasps while making this cheesecake. Start with a traditional graham cracker crust with a touch of ginger, and then the no-bake cheesecake layer. Finally, a layer of zingy blackberry sauce is swirled in on top. Perfection!

Yield: 1 (9-inch [23-cm]) round cheesecake

CRUST

1¾ cups (157 g) graham cracker crumbs

½ tsp ground ginger

¼ tsp salt

¼ cup (55 g) packed brown sugar

⅓ cup (80 ml) melted unsalted butter

BLACKBERRY SAUCE

1½ cups (216 g) blackberries

1½ tbsp (23 g) granulated sugar

1 tbsp (15 ml) water

CHEESECAKE

¾ cup (180 ml) whipping cream

2 cups (464 g) cream cheese, room temperature

⅓ cup (66 g) granulated sugar

2 tsp (4 g) lime zest (about 1 lime)

2 tbsp (16 g) powdered sugar

1 tsp vanilla extract

2 tsp (2 g) freshly grated ginger

LIME WHIPPED CREAM

1 cup (240 ml) whipping cream

2 tsp (4 g) lime zest (about 1 lime)

1 tbsp (8 g) powdered sugar

To make the crust, in a medium bowl, stir together the graham cracker crumbs, ground ginger, salt and brown sugar. Add the melted butter and mix until fully incorporated. Press the crumbs firmly into the bottom of a 9-inch (23-cm) springform pan. Transfer to the fridge or freezer to set while you prepare the cheesecake.

To make the blackberry sauce, in a medium saucepan, add the blackberries, sugar and water. Cook on medium heat for about 5 minutes, or until the berries have broken down. Blend using a small blender, and strain by pressing the mixture through a fine-mesh sieve. Transfer the mixture to a clean saucepan and cook for a few minutes on medium heat until the mixture has thickened slightly. Place in the fridge to cool while you prepare the cheesecake.

To make the cheesecake, in the bowl of a stand mixer fitted with the whisk attachment, whip the whipping cream on high for 2 to 3 minutes, until stiff peaks form. Transfer the whipped cream to a medium bowl and place in the fridge. Place the cream cheese and granulated sugar into the bowl of a stand mixer and mix on medium for about 2 to 3 minutes, or until completely smooth. Add the lime zest, powdered sugar, vanilla and fresh ginger and mix on medium for 1 to 2 minutes, or until fully incorporated. Add about one-third of the whipped cream to the cream cheese mixture and gently fold them together using a spatula. This helps lighten the texture of the cream cheese and ensures it doesn't deflate all the whipped cream. Once they are almost completely combined, add the rest of the whipped cream and continue folding until completely incorporated. Pour over the chilled crust and smooth the top. Drop several teaspoons of blackberry sauce onto the top of the cheesecake and use a knife or wooden skewer to run through them, swirling as you go. Add more sauce as needed and reserve the rest in an airtight container in the fridge to spoon over top of the cheesecake when it's ready to serve. Chill the cheesecake for 2 hours or overnight before serving.

Make the lime whipped cream directly before serving. In the bowl of a stand mixer fitted with the whisk attachment, whip the whipping cream on high for 2 to 3 minutes, or until medium stiff peaks form. Add the lime zest and powdered sugar and whip on high until incorporated. Serve the cheesecake with a dollop of the lime whipped cream and a drizzle of the reserved blackberry sauce. Store leftover cheesecake in an airtight container in the fridge for 4 to 5 days or in the freezer for 2 to 3 months.

saskatoon berry–vanilla bean grunt

Saskatoon berries are small, firm, dark berries, similar to a blueberry but a little less sweet and a little nuttier in flavor. Hard to describe really! They are commonly grown in the Canadian prairies, but we have a few rows on our farm as well. My grandpa, born in Saskatchewan, was particularly fond of them. Unlike many berries, saskatoons hold up well when cooked. And a saskatoon pie is a thing of beauty. This saskatoon grunt is even easier than pie and can be baked on the stovetop, which makes it perfect for a sticky, warm July afternoon. Biscuit dough comes together quickly and is piled on top of the berries in a cast-iron skillet. The delightful bubbling and grunting this dessert makes while baking is what gave it its name! Pop it in the oven for a minute on broil if you'd like a golden, crunchy top for the biscuits.

Yield: 1 (8- or 9-inch [20- or 23-cm]) grunt

BERRY FILLING

4 cups (592 g) saskatoon berries or blueberries

⅔ cup (132 g) granulated sugar

1 tbsp (15 ml) water

1 tsp lime juice

3" (8-cm) vanilla bean or 1½ tsp (8 ml) vanilla extract

BISCUIT TOPPING

2 cups (250 g) all-purpose flour

1 tbsp (14 g) baking powder

½ tsp salt

½ cup (114 g) unsalted butter, cold

1 cup (240 ml) whole milk

To make the berry filling, place the saskatoon berries into an 8- or 9-inch (20- or 23-cm) cast-iron skillet. Sprinkle the sugar, water and lime juice over the berries and cook on medium heat for 5 to 10 minutes, or until the berries begin to juice. Meanwhile, slice the vanilla bean in half lengthwise and scrape out the seeds using the back of a spoon. Add to the berries.

While the berries are cooking, prepare the biscuit topping. In a medium bowl, stir together the flour, baking powder and salt. Cut in the cold butter using a pastry cutter or a fork until the mixture resembles coarse crumbs. Pour the milk over and stir with a wooden spoon until it starts to come together. Dump onto a clean counter and gently pat the dough until it's 1 inch (2.5 cm) thick. Cut into circles or squares and transfer the biscuits onto the saskatoon berries that are still cooking over medium heat. Cover the skillet with a lid and the steam will cook the biscuits. Reduce the heat to low and cook for another 15 minutes, or until the biscuits look done. Try not to open the lid to peek at them before the 15 minutes are up, as the trapped steam is what is cooking them! If you wish, once the grunt has cooked, remove the lid and broil in the oven for 2 to 3 minutes, or until the biscuits get some color. Keep an eye on it the entire time! Allow the grunt to cool for a few minutes and then serve warm. Ice cream or a bit of fresh cream make excellent additions.

Seasonal Substitutes

Frozen saskatoon berries or frozen blueberries work great with this recipe!

saskatoon-studded angel food cake
with orange blossom whipped cream

Saskatoons grow in clumps similar to blueberries, but they don't ripen all at once, which makes them tough to pick quickly. They are taller than a blueberry bush and can grow to 15 or 20 feet (4.5 or 6 m)! Saskatoon berries work well when stirred into cakes and loaves, as their small size means they won't sink as much as other larger berries. They stay suspended in this beautifully fluffy angel food cake perfectly and add an unexpected pop of color. Blueberries make a great substitute if you can't find saskatoons, they just may sink a little if they're quite large.

Yield: 10–12 servings

CAKE

1½ cups (360 ml) egg whites (about 12 large eggs)

1 tsp cream of tartar

1½ cups (300 g) granulated sugar, divided

1 tsp vanilla extract

½ tsp almond extract

¼ tsp salt

1¼ cups (150 g) cake flour

1¼ cups (185 g) saskatoon berries or blueberries

WHIPPED CREAM

2 cups (480 ml) whipping cream

2–3 tbsp (16–24 g) powdered sugar

¼–¾ tsp orange blossom water, or to taste

FOR SERVING

Whipped cream or ice cream

Fresh berries

Preheat the oven to 375°F (190°C).

To make the cake, in the bowl of a stand mixer fitted with the whisk attachment, beat the egg whites and cream of tartar on medium-low for about 1 to 2 minutes, or until foamy. Increase the speed to medium and slowly add about 1 cup (200 g) of the sugar and mix until medium peaks form. Add the vanilla extract, almond extract and salt and mix briefly to combine. In a separate bowl, sift together the cake flour and remaining sugar. Gently fold the flour into the egg white mixture in three separate additions, being careful not to deflate the batter too much. Once the flour is almost completely incorporated, add the saskatoon berries and fold until distributed throughout the batter. Carefully transfer the cake batter into an ungreased angel food cake pan. Bake for 30 to 35 minutes, or until an inserted toothpick comes out clean. Rotate the cake about halfway through the bake time. Remove the cake from the oven and flip upside down onto a cooling rack, but don't remove it from the pan!

While the cake is cooling, make the whipped cream. In the bowl of a stand mixer fitted with the whisk attachment, whip the whipping cream on high for 2 to 3 minutes, until medium peaks form. Add the powdered sugar and orange blossom water to taste. Mix on high to incorporate. Keep in an airtight container in the fridge until ready to use.

Once the cake is cool (this will take a couple of hours), flip the cake back over and run a thin knife around all the edges to help it release. Flip over, tap the pan on the counter and the cake should pop right out. Serve the cake with a generous dollop of whipped cream and fresh berries. Ice cream is a great alternative too.

Note: Use a large serrated knife to gently cut the cake so that you don't squish it!

berry cheesecake no-churn ice cream

Summer months mean a lot of weed control on the farm. Seemingly endless, if I'm honest. Rows and rows of pumpkins, gourds, squash and corn need constant attention. All weeded by hand and hoe. All during the warmest months of the year. There is truly nothing sweeter than having a surprise ice cream treat dropped off by a sympathetic neighbor or friend on days like those! This no-churn ice cream is a great snack to whip up any day, and you don't need an ice cream maker to make it.

Yield: 5–6 cups (680–816 g) of ice cream

BERRY SAUCE

2 cups (246 g) raspberries

1 cup (144 g) blackberries

1 tbsp (15 ml) fresh lemon juice (about ½ lemon)

1 tsp lemon zest

2 tbsp (30 g) granulated sugar

ICE CREAM BASE

2 cups (480 ml) whipping cream

1 (14-oz [396-g]) can sweetened condensed milk

4 oz (114 g) cream cheese, room temperature

2 tsp (10 ml) vanilla extract

Pinch of salt

FOR THE TOPPING

Graham crackers, crushed

To make the berry sauce, use a blender to puree the berries with the lemon juice and zest until completely smooth. Place the berries and sugar into a small saucepan and cook on medium-low heat, stirring often, until the sauce cooks down and thickens, about 10 minutes. Remove from the heat and allow to cool completely. Strain out the seeds, if desired.

To make the ice cream base, add the whipping cream to the bowl of a stand mixer fitted with the whisk attachment. Whip on high until medium stiff peaks form. Transfer to a medium bowl and place in the fridge. (I prefer slightly under-whipping my cream. If you over-whip and move toward a butter texture, you'll end up with a very strange mouthfeel from the fat in the cream changing texture!)

In the same bowl of the stand mixer now fitted with the paddle attachment (no need to wash the bowl), mix the sweetened condensed milk, softened cream cheese, vanilla and salt on medium-low until well blended. Spoon ½ cup (120 ml) of the whipped cream into the sweetened condensed milk and use a spatula to gently fold in the whipped cream. This process helps lighten the consistency of the sweetened condensed milk mixture so it doesn't deflate the whipped cream when you combine the two. Spoon in the remaining whipped cream and fold together.

Add the berry sauce using the same folding method. For a swirled look, only fold a couple times before gently pouring the mixture into an airtight container. For a perfectly blended color, fold a few more times to distribute the sauce evenly before placing into the airtight container and transferring to the freezer. Freeze for several hours before serving. Crush a few graham crackers up and sprinkle on top. The ice cream will keep for several months in the freezer.

Seasonal Substitutes

Any kind of berry sauce will work here! Or, skip the berry sauce and stir in whatever your heart desires: caramel, chocolate, chopped Oreos, candy bar chunks, nuts, etc.

out of the orchard

Peaches, plums and pears, oh my! Summer is the gift that keeps on giving. Walking through an orchard laden with fruit is a magical sight to see. Once spring blossoms have fallen away, you can see a miniature version of the fruit to come, and the pears may be my favorite. Smaller than your thumb to start, they then swell to full size with the heat and care from their farmer. To think that these trees were bare just a few months ago and now are bursting with beautiful fruit. Pops of greens and golds, pale yellows and deep oranges, a touch of blush to royal purple. Our farm grows Black Amber and Italian plums and several different types of pears. A few wild cherry trees have also made their home in our shelter belt.

There are stone fruit in abundance. Sweet and sour cherries, baked into turnovers with a hazelnut filling (page 82) or stirred into my Cherry–Chocolate Chunk Ice Cream (page 86) for a perfectly cool treat on a warm day. Soft, ripe peaches destined for fritters (page 89) and fragrant Apricot-Blueberry Buckle (page 101) with crumble topping. Purple plums paired with warm cardamom in yummy muffins (page 98).

Let's not forget about figs, so unique in appearance and taste, and cooked into the very best jam. Then pears slip in at the end of August, tender and mellow, and wonderful when poached. They truly shine atop the Salted Caramel–Swirled Mini Pavlovas with Walnuts and Pears (page 106) and are a lovely prelude to the approaching apple season.

cherry turnovers with chocolate-hazelnut filling

There used to be a few large cherry trees at the back of one of our fields. Juicy red cherries filled their branches each year and were promptly eaten by the birds. Disappointment at its finest. Birds can be a big challenge when you grow tasty treats that they can reach faster than you can! I used sweet Bing cherries from the Okanagan Valley for these turnovers, but you can use whatever is accessible to you. Sour cherries are delicious as well. Simply toss them with ¼ cup (50 g) of sugar before adding to the turnovers. This dessert is so easy to transport and serve, which makes them perfect for picnics. No plates necessary!

Yield: about 8 turnovers

HAZELNUT SPREAD

2 cups (270 g) raw, shelled hazelnuts

⅔ cup (100 g) chopped dark chocolate

1–3 tbsp (15–45 g) granulated sugar

½ tsp vanilla extract

⅛ tsp salt

TURNOVERS

1 batch Pie Dough (page 191), divided into two disks

1 cup (296 g) hazelnut spread (see above)

2 cups (308 g) pitted, halved sweet cherries

Note: The pie crust will need to be prepared at least 1 hour before starting the pie, but preferably the day before. The crust will keep in an airtight container in the fridge for 2 to 3 days, or for up to 3 months in the freezer. Thaw in the fridge before using.

Preheat the oven to 375°F (190°C).

To make the hazelnut spread, spread the hazelnuts onto a medium rimmed baking sheet. Bake for 9 to 12 minutes, stirring a few times while baking. While the hazelnuts are roasting, melt the chocolate. Use a double boiler (see page 71) or the microwave, being sure to stir every 10 seconds. Set aside to cool slightly. Remove the hazelnuts from the oven and transfer onto a clean dish towel. Cover the hazelnuts completely with the towel and let sit for 2 to 3 minutes. This helps trap some of the steam, which softens the skin of the nuts. Gently rub with the towel to remove most of the skins. The more skins you remove, the creamier the spread will be—but it doesn't need to be perfect. Transfer the warm hazelnuts to a food processor or high-powered blender. Process on medium-low speed, stopping to stir every 15 to 20 seconds. The nuts will form a flour, then a paste and finally transform into a smooth butter. You can increase the speed throughout the process. It will take 5 to 10 minutes to get a smooth hazelnut butter. Add the melted chocolate and mix until completely incorporated. Add the sugar to taste, vanilla extract and salt. Store in an airtight container in the fridge until ready to use.

Preheat the oven to 400°F (200°C). Line a large baking sheet with parchment paper and set aside.

To make the turnovers, remove one disk of pie dough from the fridge and let rest on the counter for 15 minutes or until it's warm enough to roll out easily. On a lightly floured surface, roll the dough into a large oval or rectangle, a little larger than 12 x 24 inches (30 x 60 cm). Cut out squares with a square cookie cutter or a knife. I have a life-changing 5-wheel expandable pastry cutter that makes this a breeze, otherwise I recommend using a ruler to help keep things even. I cut 6 x 6–inch (15 x 15–cm) squares, but feel free to make them whatever size you like. Circles are fun to do as well.

(continued)

cherry turnovers with chocolate-hazelnut filling (continued)

1 egg

1 tbsp (15 ml) cream, milk or water

Coarse sugar, as needed

Once the squares are cut, place a spoonful of the chocolate-hazelnut spread near a corner, remembering that the square will be folded in half, so don't place things in its direct center. Spoon a generous number of cherries on top. Carefully fold the square in half, corner to corner, forming a triangle. Lightly wet your fingertips and run them along the inside edge of the bottom dough, and then use a fork to crimp the top edge down. The water helps the dough stick to itself. You'll want to fill the pies as full as possible without breaking the dough, and it's a process that gets easier as you work. Use a flipper to gently transfer each turnover onto the parchment-lined baking sheet. Repeat for all the dough. If you have any dough scraps left, combine them and chill them in the fridge. They can be rolled out again or saved for a small galette at a later date. Place the pan of turnovers into the freezer to chill for 15 minutes. Meanwhile, prepare the topping. In a small bowl, lightly beat an egg with 1 tablespoon (15 ml) of cream. (Milk or simply water are fine to substitute here.)

Remove the pan from the freezer and use a sharp knife to poke a few vent holes in the top of each turnover. This allows steam to escape and prevents any weird bubbling or bursting of the crust. Brush each turnover with the egg wash and sprinkle with coarse sugar. Bake for 35 to 40 minutes, or until the turnovers are golden brown and the filling is bubbling. Remove and cool on a cooling rack. Serve slightly warm or at room temperature. They're best the first day but will keep for a couple days loosely covered on the counter.

cherry–chocolate chunk ice cream

For this ice cream, you cook down cherries until they're thick and jammy, stir them into a custard base and swirl in decadent dark chocolate before freezing. Whenever you make ice cream involving fruit, it's best when served within the first couple of days, as the water content in the fruit makes it go a bit icy the longer it sits in the freezer.

Yield: 5–6 cups (680–816 g) of ice cream

CHERRY SAUCE

1½ cups (231 g) pitted, halved sweet cherries

1 tbsp (15 ml) lime juice (about 1 lime)

2 tbsp (30 g) granulated sugar

ICE CREAM BASE

1½ cups (360 ml) whole milk

1½ cups (360 ml) heavy cream

½ cup (100 g) granulated sugar

6 large egg yolks

1 tsp vanilla extract

⅛ tsp salt

MIX-INS

¼ cup (38 g) chopped dark chocolate

1 tsp coconut oil or any neutral oil

½ cup (77 g) pitted, diced sweet cherries

To make the cherry sauce, in a medium saucepan, stir together the cherries, lime juice and sugar. Cook on low heat, stirring occasionally. Mash the cherries down as they start to soften, and then carefully transfer to a high-powered blender and blend completely smooth. Use caution, as the mixture will be hot! Place the smooth cherry puree back into the saucepan and cook over medium heat until it's thick and jammy, about 5 minutes. Remove from the heat and cool to room temperature. Store in an airtight container in the fridge if not using immediately.

To make the ice cream base, in a large saucepan, stir together the milk, cream, sugar, egg yolks, vanilla and salt. Heat on medium-high, whisking constantly. Bring the mixture to 165°F (74°C) so that the yolks are safe for consumption, or until you can dip a spoon in the mixture, run your finger through the custard on the back of the spoon and it stays in place, about 10 minutes. Strain through a fine-mesh sieve to remove any stray bits of egg that may have cooked separately and allow the mixture to cool to room temperature. Stir in the cherry sauce and cool the mixture in the fridge for 2 to 3 hours or overnight. Pouring a warm mixture into an ice cream machine takes longer to freeze and can cause problems if the freezer bowl isn't cold enough to chill properly, so it's important not to skip this step.

Turn on the ice cream maker, pour in the mixture and follow the instructions given for your machine. Mine runs for about 20 to 30 minutes, and the ice cream is ready when it's incredibly thick and fluffy. To make a chocolate sauce, melt the chocolate and oil together in a bowl. I simply use a microwave and stir every 15 seconds. Adding a bit of oil to the chocolate lowers its melting point, so the chocolate softens quickly as you eat it.

Turn the ice cream maker off and remove the paddle. Use a spatula to fold in the diced cherries. You could add them earlier, but they may clog your machine if the chunks are too large. Spoon about one-third of the ice cream into an airtight container and drizzle with one-third of the melted chocolate. Spoon another third of the ice cream over and drizzle with chocolate. Repeat with the last of the ice cream and chocolate. Serve immediately as soft serve or freeze for a couple hours or up to a few weeks.

Note: Remember to place the freezer bowl of your ice cream maker into the freezer at least 24 hours before making the ice cream.

peach fritters with brown-butter glaze

At the end of each August, my dad would head to the Okanagan Valley for orchard supplies. Eventually the whole family tagged along, and we would stay for a couple of nights. We called it our great summer vacation. With a farmer's busy schedule, you learn to savor the small things, and we definitely adored those few sweet days spent swimming in the pool, playing at the beach, and picking up fresh fruit. Nothing smells better than a peach stand in late August. These peach fritters are a fun summer treat and can be served with a dusting of powdered sugar or a browned-butter glaze. As with all fritters or donuts, they're best served the same day they're made.

Yield: 12 fritters

FRITTERS

5 tbsp (71 g) unsalted butter

2¼ tsp (7 g) active dry yeast

½ tsp granulated sugar

¼ cup (60 ml) hot water

⅔ cup (160 ml) whole milk

1 large egg

¼ cup (55 g) packed brown sugar

½ tsp salt

1 tsp ground cinnamon

3–4 cups (375–500 g) all-purpose flour, divided

2 cups (308 g) chopped peaches (about 3–4 medium peaches)

Neutral oil, for frying (I like canola), at least 2½ inches (6 cm) deep depending on fry method

To make the fritters, in a medium, light-colored saucepan, brown the butter over medium heat. Using a light-colored pan helps you see what's going on at the bottom of the pan throughout the browning process. Give the pan a swirl every so often as it cooks. The butter will start to foam, and it may be hard to see the bottom. Keep swirling and cook until you can smell a nutty aroma. The browning process is cooking off excess water in the butter and browning the milk solids, which will fall to the bottom of the pan. Use a wooden spoon to move foam away to check, if necessary. Once you see little brown pieces at the bottom of the pan, 3 to 4 minutes, remove from the heat and allow to cool. Reserve 1 tablespoon (15 ml) for the glaze.

In a small bowl, stir together the yeast, granulated sugar and hot water. The water should be hot to the touch but not boiling. Let the mixture sit for about 5 minutes, or until foamy. If it never foams, try again, or you may need new yeast. In the bowl of a stand mixer fitted with the paddle attachment, stir together on medium the remaining browned butter, milk, egg, brown sugar, salt, cinnamon and 1 cup (125 g) of the flour. Add the yeast mixture and mix on medium until incorporated. Switch to the dough hook attachment. Add 1 cup (125 g) of flour and mix on low speed. The dough will likely still be quite sticky. Add more flour, 1 to 2 tablespoons (8 to 16 g) at a time, with the mixer running, until the dough pulls away from the edges of the bowl. Let the dough mix for 8 to 10 minutes on low speed. Keep an eye on it and add more flour if necessary. The goal is to have a dough that is still tacky and not perfectly smooth. I like to finish kneading by hand, but it's not necessary. The dough shouldn't cling to your hands as you knead. If it does, add a tiny bit more flour. Place the dough into a large, clean, greased bowl. Cover with a clean dish towel, and let it rise in a warm place until doubled, about 1 hour.

Meanwhile, prepare the peach filling. I prefer using peaches that aren't super ripe, as they'll be kneaded into the dough, and soft juicy pieces are tougher to work with. Peel your peaches, if desired. The easiest way to do this is by blanching them. Bring a large pot of water to a boil, and fill a large bowl with cold water and ice cubes.

(continued)

GLAZE

1 tbsp (15 ml) reserved browned butter

1½ cups (180 g) powdered sugar

1 tsp vanilla extract

1–2 tbsp (15–30 ml) cream or milk (or enough to thin out the glaze)

Seasonal Substitutes

Apples are wonderful in these fritters. Simply cook diced pieces in a frying pan with a bit of butter to soften them up before adding to the dough—otherwise they'll be a bit crunchy in the fritter!

Place the peaches into the boiling water for about a minute, remove with a slotted spoon and dunk into the ice bath. The ice bath keeps them from cooking any further. Remove from the water and set on a towel. Gently rub the peaches and the skin will slide right off. Chop the peaches into ¼-inch (6-mm) pieces and lay them out on a towel to absorb a bit of their juice.

Line a large baking sheet with parchment paper and set aside. Once the dough has risen, punch it down and turn onto a lightly floured surface. Press it into a large oval and sprinkle the peach pieces over top. Fold the edges of the dough in and gently knead together. Peach pieces will likely pop out of the dough as you work. Simply press them back in. Use a rolling pin to roll into an 9 x 12–inch (23 x 30–cm) rectangle that's about ¾ inch (2 cm) thick. This doesn't need to be exact. Cut out squares using a square cookie cutter, a pizza cutter or a knife. Mine were about 3 x 3 inches (8 x 8 cm), but you can play around with the size a little. For each fritter, bring the opposite corners together into the middle and press together, and then fold the remaining corners together over the first two, and press together firmly. Again, peach pieces may try to escape; just press them back into the dough. Transfer the folded fritter onto the parchment-lined baking sheet. Repeat the process with the remaining dough. Press any scraps together, roll them out again and repeat. Cover the fritters with a clean towel and allow them to rise for about 15 minutes while you heat up the oil.

In a deep fryer, an electric skillet or a large, heavy bottomed pan, heat the oil to 375°F (190°C). Line a wire cooling rack with a few sheets of paper towel to absorb the oil, place the rack over a large baking sheet (this will catch any large oil drips) and move it beside the fryer. If you aren't using a deep fryer with a basket, then a spider strainer works perfectly for dropping the fritters into the oil as well as removing them. When the oil is up to temperature, drop 2 to 3 fritters into the oil at a time (depending on the size of your pot). Don't crowd the fritters or it will lower the oil temperature too much and they won't cook properly. After 45 seconds of frying time, carefully check the first side of a fritter. If it's golden brown, flip it. If not, let them go for 15 to 20 seconds. You may want to try one test fritter to start with and break it open once it has cooled a bit to make sure it's cooked through. Fry each fritter for 1 minute, then flip and fry for another minute. The fritters should be golden brown when done. Remove from the oil and transfer onto the paper towel–lined cooling rack. Repeat with all the fritters. Allow to cool slightly before glazing.

To make the glaze, in a small bowl, whisk together the reserved 1 tablespoon (15 ml) of browned butter with the powdered sugar, vanilla extract and 1 tablespoon (15 ml) of cream or milk. Add more cream or powdered sugar depending on the consistency desired. Drizzle over the fritters and serve. Fritters are best served the day they're made, but they can be kept in an airtight container for 1 to 2 days at room temperature. Heat up before serving.

peach-raspberry-ginger pie

A few years ago, I decided to enter a local peach pie contest! I had never even made a peach pie before, but I thought the experience would be so fun. Peach and ginger. That was my game plan. In typical Kelsey fashion, I ran behind schedule while trying to make the pie extra fancy, and of course I decided to bake it the morning of the competition. It was still a touch warm when they cut it, and I was holding my breath as I watched! Did it set? Will it be a big mess? Lucky for me, it all worked out perfectly, and I took home second place! This is a spin on that winning pie, with raspberries added for some zinginess and color. Raspberries tend to bake up like jam in pies, which I think complements the structure provided by the sweet peach slices. A match made in heaven. Ginger adds an unexpected punch of flavor, sharp and aromatic, and it is truly what makes this pie shine. Please note that you should increase the filling by 50 percent if you're using a deep-dish pie plate that is taller than 1½ inches (4 cm).

Yield: 1 (9-inch [23-cm]) pie

PIE

About 10 peaches (5–6 cups [770–924 g] when prepared)

1 tbsp (15 ml) lemon juice

1 tbsp (15 ml) vanilla extract

½ cup (100 g) granulated sugar

⅓ cup (73 g) packed brown sugar

¼ cup (32 g) cornstarch

¼ cup (31 g) all-purpose flour

2–4 tsp (2–4 g) freshly minced ginger or ¼ tsp ground ginger (adjust depending on desired intensity)

1 batch Pie Dough (page 191), divided into two disks

3 cups (369 g) fresh or frozen raspberries

For the pie, first prepare the peaches. The easiest way to peel the peaches is by blanching them. Bring a large pot of water to a boil and fill a large bowl with cold water and ice cubes. Place the peaches into the boiling water for about 1 minute, remove with a slotted spoon and dunk into the ice bath. The ice bath keeps them from cooking any further. Remove from the water and set on a towel. Gently rub the peaches and the skin will slide right off. Cut into slices or 1-inch (2.5-cm) cubes. Drizzle the lemon juice and vanilla extract over the peaches and toss gently.

In a small bowl, stir together the granulated sugar, brown sugar, cornstarch, flour and ginger. Pour the sugar mixture over the peaches and gently stir until the peaches are coated. Transfer to the fridge while you prepare the dough.

Remove one disk of pie dough from the fridge and let it rest on the counter for about 15 minutes, or until you can roll it out without cracking. Just don't let it get too soft! Roll the dough so that it's a few inches wider than your 9-inch (23-cm) pie plate, about 12 inches (30 cm) in diameter, and carefully place it into the dish. Press along the bottom firmly to make sure the crust fits well and won't shrink when baked. Trim the outer edge if uneven. The edge should line up with the edge of the dish exactly, if you're planning on doing a braided edge. If you would prefer to crimp, leave 1 inch (2.5 cm) hanging over. Transfer to the fridge.

Repeat the above steps for a simple double-crust pie or find pie braiding instructions on page 195. Add the peach filling to the bottom crust and sprinkle the raspberries over top. Add your desired top crust and put in the freezer for 15 to 20 minutes, or until the dough is firm.

(continued)

TOPPING

TOPPING

1 large egg

1 tbsp (15 ml) cream, milk or water

Coarse sugar, as needed

FOR SERVING

Ice cream (optional)

To make the topping, in a small bowl, lightly beat the egg with the cream.

Preheat the oven to 400°F (200°C) while the pie is chilling.

When the pie has finished chilling, brush the dough with the egg wash, sprinkle with coarse sugar and immediately place into the oven. Bake for 15 minutes, and then reduce the temperature to 350°F (180°C) and bake for 45 to 50 minutes. Check on the pie as it cooks, and cover with a pie shield or a bit of aluminum foil if certain areas of the crust are getting too brown. The crust should be golden brown and the filling should be bubbling when the pie is done. Cool for 1 to 2 hours before serving so that the filling can set properly. This pie is best served with ice cream, and it's at its best the day it's made. It will keep loosely covered at room temperature for up to 2 days or a couple days longer in the fridge.

Note: The pie crust will need to be prepared at least 1 hour before starting the pie, but preferably the day before. Pie crust will keep in an airtight container in the fridge for 2 to 3 days or for up to 3 months in the freezer. (Thaw in the fridge before using.)

plum–cinnamon sugar platz

Black Amber, Early Italian, Italian, Stanley, Empress and President. Those are the plum varieties we grow, and each one is slightly different from the others. Italians are our family's favorite though. Brilliantly purple skin, with a bright yellow center. Sweet and firm. Their flavor truly can't be beat! Now you may be wondering what exactly is a platz? Platz is a thin cake piled high with fruit and topped with crumbs. It's an old Mennonite dessert, and most platz recipe cards I've looked at are pretty sparse with the instructions. Nearly all of them state "top generously with fruit" in place of the measurements, and "bake until done," which I find hilariously endearing. While both of those instructions are true, I've added a few more instructions of my own below. The wonderful thing about platz is that pretty much any fruit can be swapped in for plums, so use whatever you have on hand!

Yield: 1 (10 x 15–inch [25 x 38–cm]) cake

CAKE

2½ cups (313 g) all-purpose flour

1 cup (200 g) granulated sugar

1 tbsp (14 g) baking powder

½ tsp salt

⅔ cup (150 g) unsalted butter, softened

2 large eggs, lightly beaten

½ cup (120 ml) whole milk

1 tsp vanilla extract

3 cups (525 g) halved or sliced Italian or any variety plums

CRUMB TOPPING

½ cup (114 g) unsalted butter, softened

1 cup (200 g) granulated sugar

1 cup (125 g) all-purpose flour

¼ tsp baking powder

⅛ tsp salt

Preheat the oven to 350°F (180°C). Line a 10 x 15–inch (25 x 38–cm) rimmed jelly roll pan with parchment paper and set aside.

To make the cake, in a medium bowl, whisk together the flour, sugar, baking powder and salt. Add the softened butter with a pastry cutter until the mixture starts to resemble crumbs. Slowly stream in the beaten eggs, and then add the milk and vanilla. Use a spatula to scrape down the sides and bottom of the bowl and ensure there are no streaks of flour left. The batter will be a little lumpy, and that's just right. Pour the batter onto the prepared pan and smooth into an even layer. Place the plum halves cut side facing down onto the cake batter, or if using slices, pack close together on top of the batter.

For the crumb topping, in a small bowl, stir together the butter, sugar, flour, baking powder and salt until it resembles coarse crumbs. Sprinkle evenly over the fruit layer of the cake. Bake for 35 to 40 minutes, or until the fruit is soft and the crumbs are lightly browned. Serve warm. This will keep for a couple of days at room temperature, or freeze for a couple of months in an airtight container.

Seasonal Substitutes

Nearly any kind of fruit can be swapped in; however, rhubarb chopped into 1-inch (2.5-cm) cubes is my favorite. Halved cherries, any kind of berry or chopped peaches work as well. Frozen fruit works well too—don't defrost them before adding to the cake.

plum-cardamom muffins

A number of years ago, an 86-year-old woman decided to climb one of our plum trees, determined to reach the plums at the top! Unfortunately for her, she fell off a branch, leaving the plums out of reach and her on the ground. A few stitches later, she was good to go! But that's the reason we now have a strict "no climbing trees in the orchard" policy at the farm. I've used Black Amber and Italian plums for these muffins, but any variety of plums will work just fine. Cardamom complements the plums so well, but it can be substituted with cinnamon if you don't have cardamom on hand. I love topping all my muffins with a generous sprinkle of coarse sugar. It adds a wonderful sparkle and delicious crunch!

Yield: 12 muffins

½ cup (114 g) unsalted butter, softened

½ cup (100 g) granulated sugar

¼ cup (55 g) packed brown sugar

½ tsp almond extract

2 large eggs

2 cups (250 g) all-purpose flour

2 tsp (9 g) baking powder

½ tsp ground cardamom

½ tsp salt

½ cup (120 ml) whole milk

½ cup (120 ml) sour cream

1¼ cups (220 g) diced plums (any variety), plus extra sliced, if desired for topping

Coarse sugar, as desired

Preheat the oven to 400°F (200°C). Fill a muffin tin with liners if using or simply grease and set aside.

In the bowl of a stand mixer fitted with the paddle attachment, mix the butter, granulated sugar, brown sugar and almond extract on medium-high for 3 to 4 minutes, or until light and fluffy. Add the eggs one at a time, mixing on medium until combined.

In a medium bowl, whisk together the flour, baking powder, ground cardamom and salt. In a liquid measuring cup, stir together the milk and sour cream. Add half of the dry ingredients to the mixer, mixing on low. Follow with half the milk mixture. Scrape down the sides and bottom of the bowl, and then repeat with the remaining ingredients. Stop mixing before the batter is completely smooth as we want to avoid overmixing. Use a spatula to fold in the plum pieces. Divide the batter into the prepared muffin tin and sprinkle the tops with coarse sugar. Top with a thin slice of plum, if desired. Bake for 20 to 25 minutes, or until an inserted toothpick comes out clean. These are best served the first day, but they will keep at room temperature for up to 2 days. Freeze in an airtight container for several weeks, thaw and warm slightly before serving.

apricot-blueberry buckle

One afternoon, an employee let my dad know that our apricots were ready. My dad replied, "We don't have any apricot trees." The employee looked puzzled and told him that she was mighty certain that she ate one fresh off the tree that very afternoon. My dad went out to the orchard to see that, sure enough, three of our supposed plum trees were actually apricot trees! The trees look very similar to the plums, and it was the first year they had produced any fruit. We all had quite a laugh about it! For this buckle, I paired apricots with blueberries, and everything gets topped off with a crumb topping. Buckles aren't the prettiest of desserts, but they sure are delicious.

Yield: 1 (10-inch [25-cm]) buckle

CAKE

1½ cups (188 g) all-purpose flour

1 tsp baking powder

1 tsp baking soda

½ tsp salt

½ tsp ground ginger

½ cup (114 g) unsalted butter, softened

1 tsp vanilla extract

¾ cup (165 g) packed brown sugar

2 large eggs

½ cup (120 ml) whole milk

½ cup (120 ml) plain Greek yogurt

1 cup (148 g) blueberries

2 apricots, sliced

CRUMB TOPPING

¼ cup (60 ml) melted unsalted butter

⅓ cup (41 g) all-purpose flour

⅓ cup (73 g) packed brown sugar

½ tsp ground cinnamon

¼ cup (27 g) chopped pecans

Preheat the oven to 350°F (180°C). Grease a 10-inch (25-cm) springform or round pan and set aside.

To make the cake, in a medium bowl, whisk together the flour, baking powder, baking soda, salt and ground ginger and set aside. In the bowl of a stand mixer, mix together the butter, vanilla extract and sugar on medium-high until light and fluffy, about 2 to 3 minutes. Add the eggs one at a time, on medium until incorporated. With the mixer on low, add half of the dry ingredients and then the milk. Repeat with the rest of the dry ingredients, followed by the yogurt. Mix until just barely combined. Scrape down the sides and bottom of the bowl to ensure everything is mixed in. Fold in the blueberries. Pour the batter into the prepared pan and place the sliced apricots on top.

To make the topping, in a small bowl, stir together the melted butter, flour, sugar, cinnamon and pecans until it resembles coarse crumbs. Sprinkle over the apricots.

Bake for 45 to 55 minutes, or until an inserted toothpick comes out with just a few moist crumbs. This is best served warm the first day. It will keep for 2 days at room temperature but will get a bit soggy.

fig-oat crumble bars

I found locally grown figs at a market this summer and was hooked. I cooked mine into the fig jam that gets layered into these oat crumble bars. Skip that step and buy fig jam if figs aren't in season!

Yield: 1 (8 x 8–inch [20 x 20–cm]) pan

FIG JAM

6 cups (900 g) chopped ripe, unpeeled figs (½" [1.3-cm] pieces)

¼ cup (60 ml) water

1 cup (200 g) granulated sugar

2 tbsp (30 ml) fresh lemon juice (about 1 lemon)

1 tsp vanilla extract

BARS

1½ cups (135 g) rolled oats

¾ cup (94 g) all-purpose flour

¾ cup (94 g) spelt flour (or use all-purpose flour instead)

⅓ cup (73 g) packed brown sugar

2 tbsp (30 g) granulated sugar

½ tsp baking powder

½ tsp cinnamon

¼ tsp salt

½ cup (120 ml) melted unsalted butter

1½ cups (490 g) fig jam (see above)

Note: This jam cannot be stored at room temperature as it has not been canned. If familiar with canning, process as you would any other jam.

To make the jam, add the figs and water to a high-powered blender or food processor and blend until mostly smooth. Add the mixture to a large saucepan along with the sugar and lemon juice. Cook on medium heat, stirring occasionally, until the figs start to break down and the mixture starts to simmer. Reduce to medium-low heat and cook for about 45 to 60 minutes, until the temperature has reached 220°F (104°C), or the mixture has thickened. Stir in the vanilla extract right before pouring the jam into the jars.

While the fig jam is cooking, sterilize 3 (1-cup [240-ml]) jars. Preheat the oven to 180°F (82°C). Wash the jars and lids in hot, soapy water and rinse but do not dry. Place upside down on a clean baking sheet and bake for 15 minutes. Pour the hot jam into the hot jars. Lightly place the lids on, but do not tighten all the way. Cool to room temperature before refrigerating. Tighten the lids once cool. (Doing so beforehand makes them tighten too much.) Store in the fridge for up to 10 days or freeze up to 6 months.

Preheat the oven to 350°F (180°C). Line an 8 x 8–inch (20 x 20–cm) pan with parchment paper, leaving enough of an edge so that you'll be able to lift the bars out easily to cut.

To make the bars, in a large bowl, stir together the oats, all-purpose flour, spelt flour, brown sugar, granulated sugar, baking powder, cinnamon and salt. Add the melted butter and mix until coarse crumbs form. Press about two-thirds of the mixture into the prepared pan and bake for 10 minutes. Remove from the oven and spread the fig jam over top. Be careful as the pan will be very hot! Sprinkle the remaining crumb mixture on top. Return to the oven and bake for 20 to 25 minutes, or until the crumbs are golden brown. Remove and cool to room temperature, and then chill in the fridge until firm. Use the parchment paper to lift it out of the pan to cut into bars. Store in an airtight container in the fridge for up to a week or in the freezer for several months.

Seasonal Substitutes

Use any jam you wish for the middle layer, such as the Homemade Raspberry and Rose Jam found on page 202.

Note: Double the recipe and use a 9 x 13–inch (23 x 33–cm) pan for a larger batch, and it will use all the fig jam you will make.

gluten-free pear, hazelnut and olive oil cake

Did you know that pears don't ripen fully on the tree? It can be a little tricky to know when they're ready to harvest, as they will be firm when picked off the tree, but when you grab one and gently turn its bottom to the sky, it should let go easily. My dad always says that as soon as we see any pears on the ground, that section is ready to be picked. Most pears will ripen in about a week at room temperature and will store for longer when refrigerated. The pears and hazelnuts in this cake steal the show and create quite an eye-catching sight! The soft sweetness from the pears is complemented by the crunchy nuttiness of the nuts and is layered on top of a naturally gluten-free chocolate cake. Almond flour, bittersweet chocolate and olive oil are the secrets that lie beneath. My favorite way to serve this cake is slightly warm with a scoop of ice cream on top.

Yield: 1 (9-inch [23-cm]) round cake

¾ cup (130 g) bittersweet chocolate chips or chunks

3 eggs, divided into whites and yolks

⅔ cup (160 ml) olive oil

¼ cup (22 g) cocoa powder

½ cup (100 g) granulated sugar

½ cup (110 g) packed brown sugar

1½ cups (146 g) almond flour (or almond meal if that's what you have)

1 tsp vanilla extract

½ tsp ground ginger

½ tsp salt

3 ripe Bosc pears

½ cup (58 g) chopped raw, peeled hazelnuts

FOR SERVING

Powdered sugar (optional)

Ice cream (optional)

Preheat the oven to 350°F (180°C). Line a 9-inch (23-cm) springform pan with parchment paper and set aside.

Melt the chocolate using a double boiler. Fill a large pot with a few inches of water and bring to a boil. Place a heatproof bowl over top of the boiling water with the chocolate. The bottom should not touch the water. Stir constantly as the steam melts the chocolate. Remove from the heat and allow to cool slightly.

In the bowl of a stand mixer fitted with the whisk attachment, whip the egg whites to stiff peaks. Scrape the stiff egg whites into a clean bowl and set aside. Switch to the paddle attachment on the mixer. In the original mixing bowl (no need to clean it), place the egg yolks, oil, cocoa powder, granulated sugar, brown sugar, almond flour, vanilla extract, ginger and salt. Mix on medium until well combined. With the mixer on low, pour in the chocolate. Use a spatula to scrape down the sides and bottom of the bowl. Remove from the stand mixer and use a spatula to gently fold in the egg whites. Pour the batter into the prepared pan and smooth the surface.

Cut the pears in half, use a spoon to core and thinly slice them with a paring knife—no need to peel if you don't want to. Fan the slices out onto the top of the cake and sprinkle with chopped hazelnuts. Bake for 40 to 45 minutes, or until an inserted toothpick comes out with just a few moist crumbs. Remove from the oven and let cool for 5 to 10 minutes before carefully removing from the springform pan. This is best served a little warm and can be dusted with powdered sugar or topped with ice cream. Will keep in an airtight container in the fridge for a couple of days.

salted caramel–swirled mini pavlovas with walnuts and pears

Our pear trees tower over the dwarf apple trees and are truly beautiful. I can never decide if spring is my favorite, when the trees are bursting with blossoms, or summer, right before harvest, when the branches are heavy with fruit. Bartlett and Bosc, Comice and Conference—different shapes and sizes and slightly different flavors. Sweet and juicy, Bartletts are perhaps best for eating, although Asian pears have a lovely crunch similar to apples. Bosc remains my go-to for baking, and Comice is the least grainy of the bunch. Something for everyone! Perfectly ripe Boscs are poached with cinnamon sticks and fresh ginger for this recipe. They balance atop a caramel-swirled meringue in a beautiful cloud of whipped cream. Drizzle with more caramel if you'd like and add a few chopped nuts for a crunch. Pavlovas are great to make in summer when the air is dry and are easily customizable with any fresh fruit of the season.

Yield: 8–10 mini pavlovas

SALTED CARAMEL SAUCE

6 tbsp (84 g) unsalted butter

½ cup (120 ml) whipping cream

1 cup (200 g) granulated sugar

⅓ cup (80 ml) water

1 tsp salt

To make the salted caramel sauce, measure out all the ingredients and have them ready to go. Making homemade caramel is quite simple, but things move quickly, and it is vital that all the ingredients are ready to go. Cut the butter into tablespoon-size (14-g) chunks, and make sure it's at room temperature. Gently heat the whipping cream in a small saucepan, stirring constantly, until it is slightly warmer than room temperature. Adding ingredients to melted sugar can create problems, so bringing them to at least room temperature helps things go more smoothly!

In a medium saucepan, combine the sugar and water. Cook over medium heat, giving the pot a gentle swirl every couple of minutes to help it cook more evenly. Cook for 5 to 10 minutes, and soon you will notice a light yellow color. Keep swirling the pot occasionally and cook until the sugar turns a dark amber, but be careful not to burn it. Add the butter chunks and stir rapidly with a wooden spoon. When the butter is completely melted and incorporated, stir in the whipping cream. The mixture will bubble up quite a bit, so be careful! Keep stirring and allow the mixture to cook for 1 minute over medium heat. Remove the pan from the burner and stir in the salt. The caramel will be quite thin at this point and that's normal, as it will thicken as it cools. Let it cool to room temperature, stirring occasionally to help release heat, and then place in the fridge in an airtight container. The caramel may need to be warmed slightly before serving.

Preheat the oven to 300°F (150°C). Line one large baking sheet with parchment paper and set aside.

(continued)

MERINGUES

4 large egg whites

⅛ tsp cream of tartar

¼ tsp salt

1 cup (200 g) granulated sugar

1 tsp vanilla extract

2 tsp (10 ml) lemon juice

½ tbsp (4 g) cornstarch

¼ cup (60 ml) salted caramel sauce (see page 106)

POACHED PEARS

4 cups (960 ml) water

1 cup (200 g) granulated sugar

1" (2.5-cm) piece of ginger, minced

1 cinnamon stick

4 pears, halved and cored (I used Bosc)

WHIPPED CREAM

1 cup (240 ml) whipping cream

1 tbsp (8 g) powdered sugar

1 tsp vanilla extract

FOR SERVING

Chopped pecans or walnuts (optional)

To make the meringues, in the bowl of a stand mixer fitted with the whisk attachment, whisk the egg whites with the cream of tartar and salt on medium until soft peaks form, about 2 to 3 minutes. Add the sugar 1 tablespoon (15 g) at a time, beating well between each addition. Don't rush adding the sugar, as adding too much sugar at once can cause the meringue to deflate. Repeat until all the sugar is incorporated and the meringue forms stiff and shiny peaks, about 8 minutes. Mix in the vanilla extract, lemon juice and cornstarch, until just incorporated. Spoon the meringue onto the lined baking sheet; the size depends on your preference, but I made them roughly 5 inches (13 cm) in diameter so that half a pear would rest easily on top. Zigzag a couple teaspoons of caramel over each meringue, and then run a knife in small circles through the caramel and meringue to create swirls.

Place the meringues into the oven and immediately turn the temperature down to 250°F (120°C). Bake for 1 hour, or until the meringues are a very light cream color. Turn off the oven, leave the door cracked open and allow to cool completely inside the oven, at least 1 hour. If serving later that day, or even the next day, I will actually store my meringues in the oven and leave a note stating this on top of the oven so I don't accidentally turn it on. It's a great, dry environment for them. Meringues can also be stored in an airtight container in a cool, dry place for a couple of days before serving. They freeze very well and need only a few minutes to thaw.

While the meringues are baking, prepare the poached pears. In a large saucepan, place the water and sugar and bring to a gentle boil. Add the ginger, cinnamon stick and pears. If any of the pears are sticking out of the water, place on top a circle of parchment with the center cut out of it to create a donut shape. This will keep the pears submerged while letting the steam out. Reduce the heat to medium-low, flipping the pears occasionally, and cook for 25 to 30 minutes, or until the pears are easily pierced with a fork. Remove from the heat and let the pears cool in their liquid. Store the pears in an airtight container in their liquid in the fridge, and they will continue to soak up the flavor. Poached pears will keep for about 5 days in the fridge.

To make the topping, in the bowl of a stand mixer fitted with the whisk attachment, whip the whipping cream on high until soft peaks form. Add the powdered sugar and vanilla and mix well. Store in an airtight container in the fridge if not using immediately.

Prepare the pavlovas directly before serving. If you assemble them too much ahead of time, the whipped cream will make the meringues soggy. Top the meringues with a generous spoonful of whipped cream, a poached pear half and a drizzle of caramel sauce. Top with chopped pecans or walnuts for a great crunch, if desired.

falling for the harvest

Fall is my very favorite time of the year. It's when all of our hard work truly comes to fruition, as the apple trees come to their peak harvest, as well as our other fall crops. The mornings become a little crisper, fog may make an appearance and the leaves begin their colorful show before falling to the ground. It is the season of hot apple cider, hayrides, pumpkin picking and celebrating the harvest.

On the farm, we grow over twenty kinds of apples, ranging from sweet and juicy Honey-crisp to treasured heirloom varieties like Boskoop or Bramley. Some are great for eating and others for baking. Our personal favorites are called Elstar. Perfectly sweet and tart, they hold their shape when baking while still getting soft, and they're high in vitamin C, which keeps them from turning brown too quickly once cut. They can be a bit hard to find, but I always suggest using a tart apple whenever you bake with them.

We open our fields to the public during this season for both apple and pumpkin picking. It's so rewarding to play a small part in helping educate and connect people with where their food comes from and how it is grown. Our community is amazing!

It should come as no surprise that this chapter is a bit apple heavy. There's an Apple Slab Pie (page 121) to feed a crowd, Apple Cider Donuts (page 122) that taste like you're at an apple festival and Apple-Pecan Scones with Brown Butter Glaze (page 125) that are simple to whip up on a weekend morning. Then there are pumpkins and squash. From Mini Pumpkin Spelt Pies with Chai Whipped Cream (page 140) to Pumpkin Sourdough Loaf served warm with whipped honey butter (page 137), there's something here for everyone.

apple crisp cheesecake with salted caramel

Did you know that if you plant an apple seed, the resulting tree won't be the same variety? To grow a true variety, a bud from the desired variety is grafted onto a rootstock seedling, and that rootstock determines the size of your tree! This process can be pretty delicate, and it is a skill my dad taught me a couple of winters ago. We carefully notched seedlings, carved out buds and bound them all together. Then you pray that it all works out and that the new buds will grow. This cake is a joining of two desserts, but it requires much less finesse compared to grafting! We start with a salted caramel cheesecake base, then top it with an apple crisp made of tart apple pieces and a crumble top. Drizzle it all with caramel to finish! The great thing about this cheesecake is that there's no need to worry about it cracking, as the crisp hides all flaws.

Yield: 1 (10-inch [25-cm]) cheesecake

CRUST

1½ cups (128 g) graham cracker crumbs

2 tbsp (28 g) packed brown sugar

¼ tsp salt

¼ tsp ground allspice

¼ cup (60 ml) melted unsalted butter

CHEESECAKE

3 cups (696 g) cream cheese, room temperature

¾ cup (150 g) granulated sugar

½ cup (120 ml) full-fat plain Greek yogurt

½ cup (120 ml) salted caramel sauce (page 106), plus extra for serving, if desired

1 tsp vanilla extract

3 large eggs

Preheat the oven to 325°F (165°C).

To make the crust, in a medium bowl, stir together the graham cracker crumbs, brown sugar, salt, allspice and melted butter. Press firmly into a 10-inch (25-cm) springform pan and bake for 10 to 12 minutes, or until fragrant. Remove from the oven and set aside to cool.

To make the cheesecake, make sure the cream cheese is at room temperature, or even a bit softer, otherwise you may end up with slightly lumpy batter. In the bowl of a stand mixer fitted with the paddle attachment, mix the cream cheese and sugar on medium-low until completely smooth, 2 to 3 minutes. Add the yogurt, salted caramel sauce and vanilla extract, and mix on medium until completely combined. With the mixer on low, add the eggs one at a time, until completely incorporated. Use a spatula to scrape down the sides and bottom of the bowl throughout this process. Try not to overmix the batter and stop mixing once it's smooth. Scrape the cheesecake batter onto the crust and set aside.

(continued)

apple crisp cheesecake with salted caramel (continued)

APPLE FILLING

3–4 medium tart apples, such as
Elstar, Pink Lady or Granny Smith
(4 cups [480 g] when prepared)

½ tbsp (8 ml) lemon juice

1 tbsp (8 g) all-purpose flour

¾ tsp ground cinnamon

CRUMB TOPPING

½ cup (63 g) all-purpose flour

1 tsp baking powder

¼ tsp salt

½ tsp ground cinnamon

½ cup (110 g) packed brown sugar

¾ cup (68 g) rolled oats

¼ cup (60 ml) melted unsalted
butter

To make the apple filling, peel and chop the apples into ¼-inch (6-mm) cubes. You should have about 4 cups (480 g) of apple cubes. In a medium bowl, toss the apple pieces with lemon juice, flour and cinnamon. Spread evenly over the cheesecake layer.

To make the crumb topping, in a medium bowl, mix together the flour, baking powder, salt, cinnamon, brown sugar, oats and melted butter until coarse crumbs form. Sprinkle evenly over the apple layer.

Bake for 65 to 75 minutes, or until the apple pieces are easily pierced by a fork. If the crumb layer starts getting too brown while baking, cover with a sheet of aluminum foil. Remove from the oven when done and immediately run a thin knife along the edges to help it release from the pan. Allow to cool for 10 to 15 minutes, release the springform pan and remove. This helps the cake cool faster. Cool the cake for at least 1 hour, and then move to the fridge for several more hours or overnight before serving. Once chilled, move to an airtight container to store until ready to serve. Drizzle with additional caramel sauce, if desired. Leftovers will keep in the fridge for up to a week or in the freezer for 2 to 3 months.

Note: The caramel sauce will need to be made and cooled ahead of time if using homemade.

apple-walnut spice layer cake with swiss meringue frosting and caramel drip

If you have a backyard apple tree, then you may already know that they naturally cycle through heavy years and lighter years. This biennial bearing is how trees balance their energy, but it can be managed with pruning and thinning! We prune all our trees in winter and hand-thin every tree in spring to help even out our harvest production from year to year and to protect our trees from bearing too much fruit. This apple-and-walnut-studded spice cake is layered with brown butter swiss meringue frosting and topped off with a salted caramel drip. My ideal fall cake. If layer cakes aren't your thing, you can bake this into a 9 x 13–inch (23 x 33–cm) cake and drizzle with caramel. I always recommend baking your cake one day, storing it in the fridge overnight to chill, and then make the frosting the next day and assembling. Bite-size chunks make it easier to tackle!

Yield: 1 (6-inch [15-cm]) three-layer cake

CAKE

1 cup (227 g) unsalted butter, softened

½ cup (110 g) packed brown sugar

1 cup (200 g) granulated sugar

1 tbsp (15 ml) vanilla extract

3 large eggs

2 cups (250 g) all-purpose flour

2 tsp (9 g) baking powder

1 tsp ground cinnamon

1 tsp ground allspice

½ tsp ground ginger

¼ tsp salt

½ cup (120 ml) full-fat plain Greek yogurt

1 medium tart apple, such as Elstar, Pink Lady or Granny Smith (1 cup [125 g] when prepared)

½ cup (59 g) chopped walnuts

Preheat the oven to 350°F (180°C). Grease three 6-inch (15-cm) round cake pans with straight, 2-inch (5-cm) tall edges, and set aside. Alternatively, use two 8-inch (20-cm) pans or one 9 x 13–inch (23 x 33–cm) pan.

To make the cake, in the bowl of a stand mixer fitted with the paddle attachment, cream the butter, brown sugar, granulated sugar and vanilla extract on medium-high, until light and fluffy, about 3 to 4 minutes. Add the eggs one at a time, and mix on medium until each is fully incorporated before adding the next one. Use a spatula to scrape down the sides and bottom of the bowl. In a medium bowl, whisk together the flour, baking powder, cinnamon, allspice, ginger and salt. Add half the dry ingredient mixture to the wet ingredients and mix on low until almost incorporated, about 1 minute. Add the yogurt and mix on low. Finally, add the rest of the dry ingredient mixture, mixing on low until just combined.

Chop the apple into ¼-inch (6-mm) pieces (no need to peel it unless you want to) and measure to 1 cup (125 g). Using a spatula, fold the apple into the batter along with the chopped walnuts. Divide the batter evenly into the 3 greased cake pans. I like to use a kitchen scale to ensure the batter is distributed equally, but it's not necessary. Bake for 25 to 30 minutes, or until an inserted toothpick comes out clean. Cool for 10 minutes, and then carefully remove from the pans and cool to room temperature. If the cake layers have domed at all, you can use a long serrated knife to carefully level each one. Place the cake layers into an airtight container and chill them in the fridge before assembling. If not using right away, freeze the cake layers for up to 3 months.

(continued)

apple-walnut spice layer cake with swiss meringue frosting and caramel drip (continued)

BROWN BUTTER SWISS MERINGUE FROSTING

1 cup (227 g) unsalted butter, divided

1 tbsp (15 ml) vanilla extract

1 tbsp (15 ml) cream or milk, plus more as needed

3 cups (360 g) powdered sugar, plus more as needed

SALTED CARAMEL FILLING AND TOPPING

1 batch salted caramel sauce (recipe on page 106)

Flaked salt, coarse sugar, sprinkles, small apples, etc. (optional)

Note: If making homemade caramel sauce for this cake, it should be prepared and cooled first.

To make the frosting, you'll first brown the butter and let it cool. In a medium light-colored saucepan, heat ½ cup (114 g) of the butter on medium heat. Cut it into tablespoon-size (14-g) chunks to help it melt more evenly. Swirl the pan occasionally as it starts to cook. The butter will start to foam a couple minutes in, so keep swirling, and don't walk away from the stove. Cook 3 to 4 minutes until you start to see brown flecks on the bottom of the saucepan and a nutty aroma fills the air. Remove from the heat and cool to room temperature before transferring to the fridge. This frosting works best if the brown butter comes back to the texture of softened butter, not fully melted.

In the bowl of a stand mixer fitted with the paddle attachment, place the resolidified brown butter and the remaining butter. Whip for about 5 minutes on high. Whipping the butter for that long helps aerate it and makes it super fluffy and silky. Add the vanilla extract and the cream. Mix on low until incorporated. Add the powdered sugar and mix on medium for 1 to 2 minutes. Add more powdered sugar and/or cream until you reach the desired consistency. Store in an airtight container in the fridge or freezer until ready to assemble the cake. Bring to room temperature before using. The frosting may benefit from being re-whipped after being in the freezer.

Once the cakes are cool and level, place the first layer upside down onto your cake plate. (This reduces the number of crumbs as the cut part is facedown.) I use about 2 scoops of frosting from a 2½-inch (6-cm) ice cream scoop between each cake layer so that I know my frosting layers will be even. Spread the frosting in an even layer, and then build the frosting up slightly along the entire border of the cake layer to create a small barrier for the caramel layer. (You can omit the caramel if you wish.) Spoon a few tablespoons of salted caramel sauce on top of frosting. Repeat for the next layer. When the final cake layer is placed on top (remember to place it upside down to reduce crumbs), spread a very thin layer of frosting over the entire cake as your crumb coat. Now is a good time to check how straight your cake is standing and gently adjust the layers if possible so that it's standing straight. I like to place my cake scraper along one side and push from the other side to get it perfectly level. Move the cake into the fridge for 15 minutes or the freezer for about 10 minutes to firm up. A chilled cake is more stable, traps the crumbs in the crumb coat more efficiently and is overall easier to handle.

To frost the cake, scoop more frosting onto the chilled crumb layer and use a cake scraper (also called an icing smoother) to smooth out the frosting as you carefully spin the cake. For a more rustic look, simply add more frosting and use an offset spatula or butter knife to create swoops and swirls in the frosting. If you choose to omit the caramel drip, you could pipe more frosting on the top of the cake and decorate it however you wish.

For the caramel drip, be sure to return the cake to the fridge for another 15 minutes (or freezer for 5 to 10 minutes) so that it is properly chilled. This helps the caramel firm up once piped onto the cake. The caramel should be about room temperature, but I always recommend trying a test drip on the back of the cake to see how it reacts. Too cold and you'll get candle wax–looking drips that don't run down the cake properly, and too warm will cause the caramel to be streaky and run off the cake. Place the caramel into a squeeze bottle for easy handling or a piping bag with a very small hole or round tip. Pipe the caramel around the entire cake, pushing the caramel over the side of the cake where you want a drip. Squeeze a bit more on for a longer drip or less for a shorter drip. Fill in the top of the cake with caramel, working quickly so that it has a smooth finish, and then transfer the cake back to the fridge to help the caramel set. Top with a bit of flaked salt, coarse sugar, sprinkles, small apples, etc. Bring to room temperature before serving. Leftovers may be stored for 2 to 3 days in an airtight container in the fridge, or cut into slices and frozen for 2 to 3 months. Bring frozen pieces to room temperature before serving.

Note: The caramel drips may run slowly down the cake if kept in a warm place—not a big deal, and it will still taste great!

apple slab pie

The start of fall should always be celebrated with apple pie. How fitting is it that apple is the first pie I learned to bake? My mom walked me through the steps. Flour, fat, salt, water. A touch of sugar for a subtly sweet crust. Don't overwork it. That's just right. I always recommend using tart apples for baking, as the flavor tends to come through more! Boskoop and Bramley apples, both heirloom varieties, are wonderful cooking apples. I'll use Jonagold in a pinch and occasionally Pink Lady. Try a few out and pick your favorite. Everyone's tastes are unique and there truly is no wrong answer! This slab pie is a great way to feed a crowd, and the pieces can simply be picked up and eaten without a plate or cutlery. The biggest challenge for a slab pie can be rolling out the dough large enough and handling it as you assemble the pie. Work quickly and try not to let the dough warm up too much.

Yield: 1 (10 x 15–inch [25 x 38–cm]) sheet, about 12–15 servings

7–8 medium tart apples, such as Elstar, Pink Lady or Granny Smith (8 cups [960 g] when prepared)

1 tbsp (15 ml) lemon juice

¾ cup (150 g) granulated sugar

¼ cup (31 g) all-purpose flour

1 tsp ground cinnamon

¼ tsp ground ginger

2 batches Pie Dough (page 191), split into two large rectangles

1 large egg, lightly beaten

1 tbsp (15 ml) cream, milk or water

Coarse sugar, as desired

Note: Prepare the pie dough at least 1 hour before starting the pie, or the day before. For intricate crusts, I prefer to have lots of extra dough to work with. Dough will keep in an airtight container in the fridge for 2 to 3 days or for up to 3 months in the freezer. (Thaw in the fridge before using.)

Peel and chop the apples. You should have around 8 cups (960 g). Place the chopped apple pieces in a large mixing bowl and drizzle with lemon juice to help keep them from browning too much. In a small bowl, mix together the sugar, flour, cinnamon and ginger. Add the mixture to the apples and toss until the apples are evenly coated. Set aside.

Remove one pie crust rectangle from the fridge and let it rest on the counter for about 15 minutes, or until you can roll it out without cracking; just don't let it get too soft! Roll the dough so that it's a couple of inches wider than the 10 x 15–inch (25 x 38–cm) rimmed baking sheet. This can be tough to roll out and will not be perfect. If the shape gets lopsided, trim the edges and press them together in a spot that needs more dough. Transfer to the baking sheet, add the apple filling and move to the fridge. Roll out the second rectangle of dough the same way. For a simple top crust, use the dough as is and drape the rolled-out piece over the apple filling, crimping the edges to seal. Cut a few vent holes in the top crust to let the steam escape when baking. For lattice instructions, see page 192, and for braid instructions, see page 195. Transfer the pie to the freezer (if you have room) or fridge for 15 to 20 minutes, or until the dough is very firm.

Preheat the oven to 425°F (220°C).

In a small bowl, lightly beat the egg with the cream. Remove the pie from the freezer, and brush the top of the dough with the egg wash and sprinkle with coarse sugar. Bake for 15 minutes, and then reduce the oven temperature to 350°F (180°C) and bake for 40 to 50 minutes. The pie is done when the apples are soft when poked and the crust is golden brown. If the crust starts to get a bit dark while cooking, cover with a bit of aluminum foil. Remove from the oven and allow to cool on a cooling rack for about 1 hour before serving. The pie is best served the first day but will keep loosely covered for 2 more days.

apple cider donuts

Warmed up with cinnamon, nutmeg and cloves, our farm's hot cider tastes like autumn in a cup. We don't sell donuts on the farm, but if we did, these apple cider ones would be it. First you reduce fresh apple cider down until it's thick and syrupy. Then you prepare the batter, chill, roll out, fry and roll in a spiced sugar mixture.

Yield: 6–7 donuts

DONUTS

1½ cups (360 ml) apple cider

¼ cup (55 g) packed brown sugar

¼ cup (50 g) granulated sugar

1 tsp baking powder

⅛ tsp salt

1 tsp ground cinnamon

½ tsp ground allspice

2¼ cups (286 g) all-purpose flour

¼ cup (60 ml) melted unsalted butter

Neutral oil, for frying (I like canola), amount will vary depending on fry method

TOPPING

½ cup (100 g) granulated sugar

1 tbsp (8 g) ground cinnamon

In a medium saucepan, bring the apple cider to a gentle boil over medium-high heat. Reduce to a simmer, stirring occasionally, and reduce the apple cider down until ½ cup (120 ml) of liquid remains. This will take about 15 to 20 minutes.

In a medium bowl, whisk together the brown sugar, granulated sugar, baking powder, salt, cinnamon, allspice and flour. Make a well in the middle and pour in the melted butter and reduced apple cider. Stir with a wooden spoon until the batter comes together. It will be thick and shaggy. Dump out onto a lightly floured surface and gently press together until the dough is combined. Press into a ½-inch (1.3-cm) slab. Cut out the donuts. Gather scraps of dough and press together again to cut out more donuts.

In a deep fryer, an electric skillet or a large, heavy bottomed pan, heat the oil to 375°F (190°C). Line a wire cooling rack with a few sheets of paper towels to absorb the oil, place the rack over a large baking sheet (this will catch any large oil drips) and move it beside the fryer. If you aren't using a deep fryer with a basket, then a spider strainer works perfectly for dropping the donuts into the oil as well as removing them. When the oil is up to temperature, drop 2 to 3 donuts into the oil at a time (depending on the size of your pot). Don't crowd the donuts or it will lower the oil temperature too much and they won't cook properly. You may want to try one test donut to start with and break it open once it has cooled a bit to make sure it's cooked through. Fry each donut for 1 to 2 minutes, and then flip and fry for another 1 to 2 minutes. Donuts should be golden brown when done. Remove from the oil and transfer onto the paper towel–lined cooling rack. Repeat with all the donuts. Let each donut cool until you can touch them.

To make the topping, mix together the sugar and cinnamon in a small bowl, and then dip the donuts into the cinnamon sugar. Serve immediately. These donuts are best served warm. Store in an airtight container for up to 2 days and warm slightly before serving.

Note: What's the difference between fresh apple cider and apple juice? Fresh apple cider is simply the freshly pressed juice from apples and will have a cloudy appearance and a more robust flavor. Apple juice has been filtered, clarified and processed.

apple-pecan scones with brown butter glaze

Early mornings in late September spent on a ladder in our foggy orchard, picking apple after apple, is one of the most magical places to be. All of our apples are handpicked into large, tube-like bags. You fold the bottom of the bag up and hook it to the top while you pick, so the apples don't fall out. Then you unhook and gently let the apples roll into the bin when your bag is full. Over and over until it's full. Just like apples, this scone dough is best when handled delicately. I like to gently fold mine together, allowing it to be a bit shaggy rather than risk overmixing it and getting tough scones. They are packed full of diced apples, and I recommend using a tart variety that holds its shape when baked, such as Elstar, Pink Lady or Braeburn. The pecans give them the perfect amount of crunch, and a brown butter glaze is always a good idea.

Yield: 8–12 scones

SCONES

2¼ cups (286 g) all-purpose flour

½ tsp baking soda

2 tsp (9 g) baking powder

⅛ tsp cream of tartar

¼ tsp salt

½ tsp ground cinnamon

½ cup (110 g) packed brown sugar

½ cup (114 g) unsalted butter, chilled

1 cup (125 g) peeled and chopped tart apple (about 1 medium apple cut into ½-inch [1.3-cm] cubes)

½ cup (55 g) chopped pecans

½ cup (120 ml) whole milk, plus extra for topping

1 large egg

1 tsp vanilla extract

Coarse sugar, as needed

GLAZE

2 tbsp (30 ml) melted butter, browned (see page 118)

1½ cups (180 g) powdered sugar

1 tsp vanilla extract

1–2 tbsp (15–30 ml) cream or milk, as needed

Preheat the oven to 400°F (200°C). Line a 10 x 15–inch (25 x 38–cm) baking sheet with parchment paper or a silicone baking mat. Set aside.

In a medium bowl, whisk together the flour, baking soda, baking powder, cream of tartar, salt, cinnamon and brown sugar. Cut the butter into the dry ingredients with a pastry cutter or a fork. Work until the butter pieces are all about the size of a pea. Add the apple and pecan pieces and toss. Place the bowl in the freezer to keep cold.

In a medium bowl, whisk the milk, egg and vanilla extract together until fully mixed. Remove the bowl from the freezer and pour the wet ingredients over top. Gently stir together until a shaggy dough forms. Pour onto a clean counter and gently press the dough together. For large scones, press into an 8-inch (20-cm)-wide circle and cut into 8 triangles. For small scones, divide the dough into two 5-inch (13-cm) circles and cut each into 6 scones. Brush the tops with milk and sprinkle with coarse sugar for some sparkle and texture. Bake until the scone tops are light brown. For large scones, bake for 18 to 20 minutes, and for smaller scones, bake for 16 to 18 minutes. I always recommend baking a test scone to make sure the bake time is right.

While the scones are baking, make the glaze. In a medium bowl, whisk together the browned butter (see page 118 for the method), powdered sugar and vanilla. Add 1 to 2 tablespoons (15 to 30 ml) of milk to thin, if necessary. Drizzle the glaze over the hot scones to encourage the glaze to soak in, or wait until the scones have cooled more. Best served slightly warm. These will keep in an airtight container for 1 to 2 days or can be frozen for 2 to 3 months. Thaw and warm to serve.

Seasonal Substitutes

Swap in blueberries in summer or cranberries in winter. Skip the brown butter portion of the glaze and replace with 2 tablespoons (30 ml) of lemon juice and zest from 1 lemon for a zingy glaze.

apple cider ice cream with oat crumble

Apple cider slushies are possibly our most popular treat on the farm. Pure apple cider is simply poured into a slushie machine, and bam! The perfect frozen treat. We decided to try it out one year with our farm's fresh cider, and my dad declined the sugar-y syrup that we were advised to add to it to keep it from freezing solid. "Apples have enough natural sugars in them, it'll be fine," he huffed. And it turns out that he was right! A local ice cream shop used the same principle when they came up with a soft apple cider ice cream made with our farm's cider, and they kindly gave me the go-ahead to share my own take on this idea. (Thanks, Banter Ice Cream!) I added a crunchy, spiced oat crumble to give it a little texture, which can be served on the side to sprinkle on top or mixed right into the ice cream before it's fully set in the freezer. Now, it's not a slushie . . . but it's a lovely treat for those warm early fall days.

Yield: about 5 cups (680 g) of ice cream

ICE CREAM

6 egg yolks

1½ cups (360 ml) apple cider

1½ cups (360 ml) whipping cream

1½ cups (360 ml) whole milk

2–4 tbsp (30–60 g) granulated sugar, or to taste

¾ tsp ground cinnamon

½ tsp ground ginger

½ tsp ground allspice

Pinch of salt

In a small bowl, whisk together the egg yolks and set aside. In a large saucepan, bring the apple cider to a gentle simmer over medium heat, stirring occasionally. Cook down, stirring more often as the cider gets thicker, until it has reduced to about ½ cup (120 ml). Slowly stream in the cream and then the milk, continuing to stir. Heat until the mixture begins to steam. Remove about ½ cup (120 ml) of the warm liquid and very slowly stream it into the bowl with the egg yolks, whisking continuously. Once fully incorporated, stream in another ½ cup (120 ml) of warm liquid. This helps bring the egg yolks up to temperature without cooking them into a lumpy mess. Then whisk the warmed egg yolk mixture back into the saucepan with the rest of the liquid. Heat on medium-high, whisking continuously. Bring the mixture to 170°F (77°C), as this ensures your yolks are safe to eat, or until you can dip a spoon into the mixture and run your fingers through the custard ice cream base without it running, about 10 minutes.

When the mixture reaches 170°F (77°C), stir in 2 tablespoons (30 g) of sugar. Taste the mixture and add more sugar if you would like it sweeter. Continue heating until the sugar is completely dissolved. Stir in the cinnamon, ginger, allspice and salt. Remove from the heat and cool the mixture by setting the saucepan into a bath of ice water and stirring occasionally to release the heat. Once the mixture has reached room temperature, you can chill it in the fridge for several hours or place directly into your ice cream maker (if you're impatient like me) and follow your machine's instructions. My ice cream maker takes 20 to 30 minutes, and the texture gets quite thick.

(continued)

OAT CRUMBLE

⅓ cup (73 g) packed brown sugar

2 tbsp (30 g) granulated sugar

⅔ cup (83 g) all-purpose flour

⅔ cup (59 g) rolled oats

¼ cup (60 ml) melted unsalted butter

1 tsp ground cinnamon

¼ tsp salt

While the ice cream maker is running, make the oat crumble. Preheat the oven to 350°F (180°C). Line a medium rimmed baking sheet with parchment paper and set aside.

In a medium bowl, stir together the brown sugar, granulated sugar, flour, oats, melted butter, cinnamon and salt. Use your hands to press some of the crumb mixture together to make clumps and sprinkle them evenly over the prepared baking sheet. Bake for about 15 to 17 minutes, stirring every 5 minutes, until golden brown. Remove from the oven, place the pan on a wire cooling rack and allow to cool completely.

When the apple cider ice cream has finished churning, it can be served immediately as soft serve or placed into an airtight container and firmed up for a couple of hours before serving. Oat crumble can be served by sprinkling it on top of the ice cream or swirled right into it. To swirl the oat crumble into the ice cream, spoon about one-quarter of the ice cream directly from the machine into an airtight container and sprinkle crumbs on top, and repeat. Then place into the freezer to firm up. Best if served within the first week. If the ice cream does harden up, it may need 10 to 15 minutes on the counter to make scooping easier.

apple puff pastry rose tarts

I spend a lot of time with our apple trees and often refer to them as my babies. From spring planting to winter pruning, you can usually find me tying up branches, thinning excess fruit and harvesting. We train our trees to grow in an "S" shape in order to encourage branching and fruit production, which requires careful shaping during the first few years after planting. This shaping must be done when the trunks are young and flexible so the branches don't break! The same care must be taken when shaping these tarts, and the apple slices will require a short boil for them to roll without cracking. When rolled into puff pastry, they create a lovely rose-shaped tart. I used Pink Lady apples as they don't brown easily, they have bright red skin and their tart flavor works well when baked. If you can find a pink-fleshed apple, I think that would be lovely, too. These tarts work equally well with persimmon, which is a lovely autumnal fruit that is often overlooked!

Yield: 12 puff pastry roses

CHAI SPICE BLEND

1 tbsp (8 g) ground cinnamon

1 tbsp (5 g) ground ginger

1 tsp ground cardamom

½ tsp ground cloves

½ tsp ground nutmeg

TARTS

4 medium tart baking apples (I used Pink Lady)

2 sheets frozen puff pastry, thawed for 2 hours before use

¾ cup (170 g) unsalted butter, softened, divided

½ cup (100 g) granulated sugar

½ tbsp (4 g) chai spice blend (see above), divided

Powdered sugar, for serving

To make the chai spice blend, in a small bowl, mix together the cinnamon, ginger, cardamom, cloves and nutmeg. Set aside. (You will have extra after this recipe, which you can add to warm drinks, oatmeal and cakes and loaves. You can also mix it with sugar to roll donuts or soft pretzels!)

Preheat the oven to 375°F (190°C). Grease a muffin tin with butter or cooking spray and set aside. Heat a large, wide saucepan filled with several inches of water over medium heat until it comes to a simmer. Cut each apple in half and carefully carve out the core with a paring knife. Place the flat side down, and starting at the stem's edge, slice the apple horizontally into the thinnest slices you can manage. Since the apple slices will be rolled up in the pastry, the thinner the better. Work quickly to avoid browning and move all the apple slices into the pot of simmering water. Cook for 2 to 4 minutes or until the apples bend instead of breaking when you curve them into a circle. Remove from the heat, carefully strain and place onto a towel to dry.

To make the tart, keep one sheet of puff pastry in the fridge as you start to work with the other. Warm puff pastry dough is tough to work with. Roll out one sheet of puff pastry to a 12 x 10–inch (30 x 25–cm) rectangle, leaving it on the parchment it comes on for easy transfer and cleanup. With the 12-inch (30-cm) side closest to you, use a pizza cutter or sharp knife to cut 6 equal strips, each 2 inches (5 cm) wide. Spread ¼ cup (57 g) softened butter onto the entire sheet in a thin layer.

In a small bowl, mix together the sugar and ½ tablespoon (4 g) chai spice blend and sprinkle a generous amount over the softened butter.

(continued)

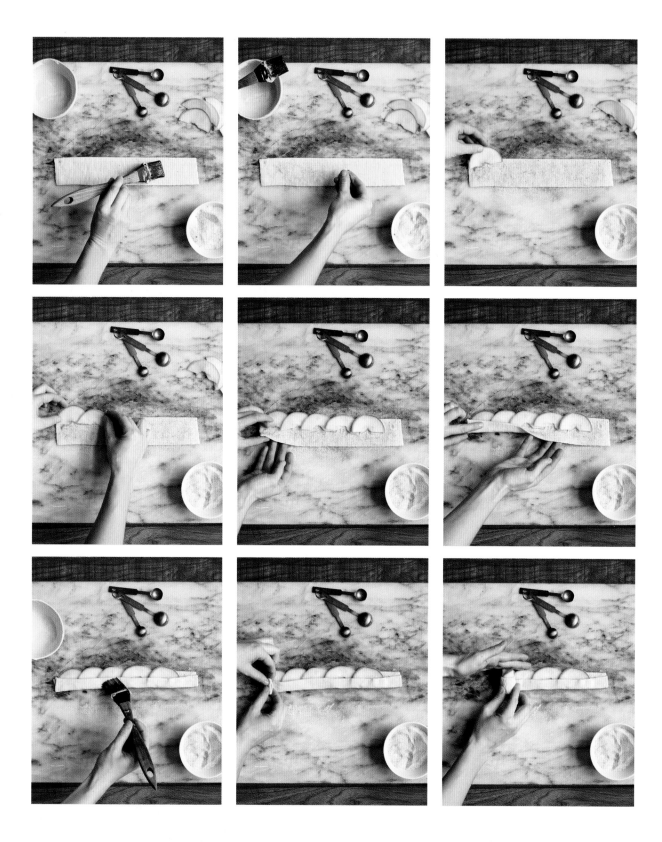

apple puff pastry rose tarts (continued)

Start the first strip with the thinnest apple slice, as it will form the middle of the rose and will need to be the most flexible. Place the apple about halfway down the puff pastry strip with the skin side poking up over the dough.

Place a second apple slice over the first, overlapping about one-quarter of a slice. Repeat until you reach the end of the dough.

Carefully fold the half of the strip without apple slices on it over top of the apples.

You may want to use a butter knife or offset spatula to help lift the dough off the parchment. If the dough ever gets too soft, sticky or difficult to work with, simply place back into the fridge for 5 minutes. Melt ¼ cup (57 g) of butter. Once the dough has been folded up, brush the edge with some of the melted butter.

Then roll the strip up as tightly as you can.

Press the end of the strip firmly into the rest of the dough and transfer the rose to the prepared muffin tin. Repeat for the remaining 5 strips of dough. Transfer the muffin tin to the fridge to stay cool, and repeat the above steps with the second sheet of puff pastry.

Bake for 35 to 40 minutes, or until the pastry is puffed and golden. Rotate the muffin tin halfway through baking and peek in on the roses to make sure the top of the apples don't burn. Place a bit of aluminum foil on top if the apples are cooking too quickly. Cool on a cooling rack for about 5 minutes, and then carefully remove the roses from the muffin tin. Top with powdered sugar and serve. These are best served the first day, but you can keep them in an airtight container for a couple of days.

puff pastry rose tarts with persimmon

6 ripe persimmons

1 cup (325 g) blackberry or any flavor jam

2 tsp (3 g) chai spice blend (page 130)

Cut each persimmon in half and remove the stem. Place the flat side down and starting at the stem edge, slice the persimmon horizontally into the thinnest slices you can manage. Persimmons are more flexible than apples and don't need to be boiled at all to be flexible enough. Follow the rest of the steps of the apple version, but stir together the blackberry jam and chai spices and substitute it for the butter-sugar filling, if desired.

pumpkin cheesecake with gingersnap crust and toasted meringue

Growing up on a pumpkin farm meant that I didn't realize you could buy pumpkin puree at the store until I was an adult. These days, I can understand the convenience of buying the canned version, but I urge everyone I meet to try making their own. This pumpkin cheesecake is one of my very favorite recipes of all time, as it combines my deep love for pumpkin with a homemade gingersnap crust and a beautiful toasted meringue top. Prepare a few days ahead of time (minus the meringue) if you'd like, and torch the meringue at the table to really impress your friends!

Yield: 1 (8-inch [20-cm]) cheesecake

GINGERSNAP CRUST

2 cups (336 g) crushed homemade or store-bought gingersnap cookies

6 tbsp (84 g) unsalted butter

⅛ tsp salt

CHEESECAKE

2 cups (464 g) cream cheese (2 packages), room temperature

½ cup (100 g) granulated sugar

1 cup (245 g) Pumpkin Puree (page 205)

1 tsp vanilla extract

2 tbsp (16 g) all-purpose flour

½ tsp ground cinnamon

½ tsp ground allspice

2 large eggs, room temperature

1 large egg yolk, room temperature (reserve white to use for meringue)

Preheat the oven to 350°F (180°C).

To make the crust, place the gingersnap cookies into a food processor or blender and blend into fine crumbs. I did this ½ cup (84 g) at a time. Repeat until you have 2 cups (336 g) of fine crumbs.

In a medium bowl, stir together the gingersnap crumbs, butter and salt. Press firmly into the bottom of an 8-inch (20-cm) springform pan. Bake for 8 to 10 minutes, or until fragrant. Set aside to cool.

To make the cheesecake, preheat the oven to 260°F (130°C). Cooking a cheesecake at a low temperature decreases the chance of it cracking, and I've never had a cracked cake using this method! In the bowl of a stand mixer fitted with the paddle attachment, beat together the cream cheese and sugar on low for 1 to 2 minutes, until completely smooth. Make sure the cream cheese is at room temperature or the batter will have small lumps in it. Add the pumpkin puree, vanilla, flour, cinnamon and allspice and beat on low for 2 minutes, until smooth. Use a spatula to scrape down the sides of the bowl and gently run it through the batter to press some of the air bubbles out. Add the eggs one at a time, mixing until barely mixed, and then add the yolk and beat on low until just incorporated. Use a spatula to scrape down the sides and press out any air bubbles. Try not to overmix once the eggs are added.

(continued)

MERINGUE

½ cup (120 ml) egg whites (about 4 eggs)

1 cup (200 g) granulated sugar

1 tsp vanilla extract

Pour the batter into the cooled crust and slam the entire pan down onto the counter firmly several times. You should see a few air bubbles pop on the surface. We don't want these bubbles rising through the batter while it bakes, as they can create a bumpy surface.

Bake for 55 minutes, and then turn off the oven, crack the door and let the cheesecake rest in the oven for 15 to 20 minutes. Remove from the oven, run a thin knife around the edge and leave in the pan for at least 1 hour. Carefully remove the springform pan wall piece and let the cheesecake come to room temperature before placing into the fridge in an airtight container. Allow to chill for several hours or overnight. This cake is great to make a day or two before you need it.

To make the meringue topping, ensure that a small saucepan and the mixing bowl of the stand mixer are freshly washed and dried and free from any grease. In the saucepan, whisk together the egg whites and sugar. Assemble a double boiler by bringing a large pot of water containing a couple inches of water to a boil, and place the saucepan with the egg whites and sugar on top. Make sure the bottom of the saucepan doesn't touch the water. Stir occasionally and heat until the mixture reaches 160°F (71°C). Keep cooking at that temperature for a couple of minutes. Since we aren't cooking the meringue after it's made, this process is ensuring the eggs are safe to eat. Remove from the heat and place the mixture into the bowl of a stand mixer fitted with the whisk attachment. Beat on medium-low for 4 minutes while the egg mixture cools, and then increase the speed to high for 4 minutes. Beat until it forms a thick and glossy meringue. Mix in the vanilla extract. Use immediately.

The cheesecake should be well chilled before serving and the meringue assembled directly before serving. Pile the cheesecake high with meringue and use a kitchen torch to toast the meringue. If you don't have a kitchen torch, you can broil the cake for a few minutes, but keep an eye on it the entire time! Alternatively, serve with whipped cream. Store leftovers in an airtight container for 2 to 3 days in the fridge or for 3 months in the freezer. The meringue will get a bit soggy after the first day.

Note: If using homemade gingersnaps that are on the soft side, chop into fine pieces and spread onto a parchment-lined baking sheet. Bake until dry and crunchy, stirring every few minutes. Allow to cool slightly and then blend into fine crumbs.

pumpkin sourdough loaf with whipped honey butter

My sister, Jordyn, started her sourdough journey a while ago, and she's been churning out loaf after loaf of delicious, bready goodness ever since. Our whole family has truly benefited from this hobby. I always joke that she's the true baker between the two of us . . . I mean, she has even started making her own cheese, for goodness' sake. I knew I wanted to ask her to collaborate on a recipe for this book, and here it is. Pumpkin sourdough by Jordyn. Whipped honey butter by me. Seriously, this is a match made in heaven. The sourdough has the loveliest orange tint and is so perfect for the season. Top it with the dreamiest whipped butter sweetened with honey and sprinkled with cinnamon, if you please.

Yield: 1 loaf

PUMPKIN SOURDOUGH

1¼ cups (306 g) Pumpkin Puree (recipe on page 205)

⅔ cup (160 g) sourdough starter

1½ cups (206 g) bread flour

1½ cups (188 g) all-purpose flour

1 tsp salt

To make the pumpkin sourdough, in a large bowl, mix together the pumpkin puree and active sourdough starter. It will work best if both are at room temperature. Once thoroughly combined, add the bread flour, all-purpose flour and salt. Mix until all of the ingredients are incorporated, and then turn the dough out onto a clean surface. Knead for 8 to 10 minutes, or until the dough is smooth. The dough will start out super sticky—that's normal. A flexible dough scraper is super handy for this step. You can use it to scrape the dough up and over itself, and repeat. Try not to add any extra flour during the kneading process. The bread will come together as you continue to knead. Once you have a smooth and elastic dough, form it into a ball and place it back in the bowl to rise. Cover with a clean dish towel or lid and let it rise for 3 to 3½ hours. The dough should look puffy but not doubled in size. During the colder months, it may require a bit more time to rise, and during the warmer months, a bit less.

Turn the dough out onto a lightly floured surface. Start with the edge farthest from your body, and pull the dough to the center and press firmly. Repeat three times, clockwise around the dough. Flip the dough so the seams sit on the counter. To shape your dough into a ball, use your hands to gently cup the dough and pull it toward you in a straight line. Rotate it 45 degrees and repeat until a ball forms. This becomes clearer once you start working the dough. Place in an 8-inch (20-cm) round floured banneton or in a medium bowl lined with a floured tea towel. Cover with plastic wrap or fold the tea towel over itself so no bread is exposed. Place in the fridge overnight.

(continued)

WHIPPED HONEY BUTTER

1 cup (227 g) salted butter

¼ cup (60 ml) liquid honey

FOR SERVING

Ground cinnamon (optional)

Note: Don't have any sourdough starter? There are so many great books and blogs that lead you through the process of starting your own. If you're lucky, you may have a baker friend who will gift you some or a local bread shop may sell some! You can also find dried starter online along with instructions on how to care for it.

While the bread is rising, prepare the whipped honey butter. In the bowl of a stand mixer fitted with the whisk attachment, mix together the butter and honey on medium-high for 3 to 5 minutes. Store the butter in an airtight container in the fridge.

In the morning, place a large (mine is 1.4-gallons [5.3-L]), cold Dutch oven with a lid into the cold oven and preheat to 400°F (200°C), for 30 minutes. This is a very important step and should never be skipped! When the Dutch oven is hot, remove the bread from the fridge and turn it out onto a large square of parchment paper. Use your fingers to smooth out any spots of flour that stuck to the loaf from the banneton. Then dust the top of the bread with flour so that it is evenly covered. Dusting the loaf with flour helps maximize the contrast between the flour and the crust that is revealed by scoring and darkens when baked. Score the bread with a lame or a very sharp knife. Scoring is simply cutting the bread with a sharp blade and is important for helping the bread expand while baking. Different sizes and shapes of cuts will affect the shape of the bread.

For the next steps, silicone baking mitts are recommended to make everything easier to handle and to keep your hands nice and safe. Take the hot Dutch oven out of the oven, remove the lid and gently pick up the corners of the parchment paper to pick up the bread and transfer it to the Dutch oven. Replace the Dutch oven lid and place the Dutch oven back into the hot oven. Bake with the lid on for 25 minutes, remove the lid and bake for 20 minutes. Remove from the oven and let it cool completely before slicing with a sharp bread knife. Serve with the whipped honey butter and a dash of cinnamon, if desired.

mini pumpkin spelt pies with chai whipped cream

These mini pumpkin pie tarts are cute as can be and are a fun change from a traditional pumpkin pie. Small pies mean a high crust ratio! Chai-spiced whipped cream tops things off with a creamy texture.

Yield: 18–24 mini pies

PUMPKIN PIE

½ batch Pie Dough with spelt flour variation (page 191)

2 cups (490 g) Pumpkin Puree (page 205)

2 large eggs

2 large egg yolks

⅓ cup (66 g) granulated sugar

⅓ cup (73 g) packed brown sugar

1 cup (240 ml) whipping cream

½ tsp salt

2 tsp (3 g) ground cinnamon

¾ tsp ground ginger

½ tsp ground allspice

⅛ tsp ground cardamom

CHAI WHIPPED CREAM

1 cup (240 ml) whipping cream

1 tbsp (8 g) powdered sugar, plus extra if needed

1 tsp chai spice blend (page 130), plus extra if needed

Preheat the oven to 400°F (200°C).

To make the pie, remove the disk of pie dough from the fridge and let it rest on the counter for about 15 minutes, or until you can roll it out without cracking; just don't let it get too soft! Roll the dough out on a lightly floured surface. Use a round cookie cutter between 4 and 5 inches (10 and 13 cm) in diameter to cut out rounds. You can use a fluted cookie cutter for a fancier edge. Transfer each dough round to a muffin tin and gently but firmly press in the dough. Repeat with all the dough. Transfer to the fridge or freezer to chill until firm, 5 to 10 minutes.

Cut out decorative leaves from any leftover dough, if desired, and transfer the dough leaves to a small parchment-lined baking sheet and freeze for 10 to 15 minutes, or until the dough is completely firm. Score the frozen leaves with a small knife to add detail if you'd like. Bake for 10 to 15 minutes, or until golden brown. Small cutouts can brown or burn quickly, so keep an eye on them the entire time. Set aside to cool. I like to bake these before the pie goes in the oven, as they don't take very long.

In the bowl of a stand mixer fitted with the paddle attachment, mix together the pumpkin puree, eggs, egg yolks, granulated sugar and brown sugar on medium until smooth. With the mixer on low, stream in the whipping cream. Add the salt, cinnamon, ginger, allspice and cardamom and mix on low until smooth. Use a spatula to scrape down the sides and bottom of the bowl to ensure everything is well mixed. Fill each muffin cavity two-thirds full, as the filling will puff slightly when baked. Extra pie shells can be baked and saved for later. (They make great ice cream boats.) Or, you can press them back together and refrigerate to use for a galette later on. Bake for 20 to 25 minutes, or until the crust looks golden. Remove and cool for 5 to 10 minutes before carefully removing from the muffin tin. Transfer to the fridge to chill before serving. Store in an airtight container.

To make the whipped cream, in the bowl of a stand mixer fitted with the whisk attachment, whip the whipping cream on high until medium peaks form, about 2 to 4 minutes. Add the powdered sugar and chai spices and whip until incorporated. Add more sugar or spice as needed. Serve chilled pies with a generous dollop of spiced whipped cream and a decorative leaf on top. Store extras in the fridge.

Note: The pie dough will need to be prepared at least 1 hour before starting the pie but preferably the day before.

pumpkin loaf—3 ways

Every fall, my parents have a giant pumpkin growing contest between them! Well, my dad used to simply plant his and walk away . . . which led to my mom winning year after year. I joined his team a few years ago, and to my mom's dismay, we beat her with a gorgeous, bright orange 817-pound (371-kg) Atlantic Giant. Some may call it beginners' luck, but my dad and I won again two years later with a whopper that weighed over 1,000 pounds (454 kg)! However, I do need to admit that my mom helps me out with growing more than Dad does! Giant pumpkins may be good for bragging rights and for making a boat . . . but not so much for baking with. Stick to the smaller, sweeter varieties for that. This pumpkin loaf is a choose-your-own-adventure bread, as I've included three different ways to make it while encouraging you to put your own spin on them.

Yield: 1 (5 x 9–inch [13 x 23–cm]) loaf

PUMPKIN LOAF BASE

2 large eggs

¾ cup (150 g) granulated sugar

¼ cup (55 g) packed brown sugar

½ cup (120 ml) vegetable oil

1 cup (245 g) Pumpkin Puree (page 205)

½ tsp baking soda

½ tsp baking powder

1 tsp salt

2 cups (250 g) all-purpose flour

1 tsp ground cinnamon

½ tsp ground ginger

¼ cup (60 ml) full-fat sour cream

¼ cup (60 ml) milk

LOAF VERSION 1

⅓ cup (66 g) granulated sugar

1 tbsp (8 g) cinnamon

LOAF VERSION 2

⅔ cup (117 g) chocolate chips

LOAF VERSION 3

⅓ cup (48 g) craisins

⅓ cup (36 g) chopped pecans

Preheat the oven to 350°F (180°C). Grease a 5 x 9–inch (13 x 23–cm) loaf pan and set aside.

In the bowl of a stand mixer fitted with the paddle attachment, combine the eggs, granulated sugar, brown sugar, oil and pumpkin puree. Mix on medium-low until fully incorporated. In another large mixing bowl, whisk together the baking soda, baking powder, salt, flour, cinnamon and ginger. Set aside. In a liquid measuring cup, measure out the sour cream and milk and stir. Add half of the flour mixture to the pumpkin mixture and mix on low until barely combined. Streaks of flour should remain. Add the milk mixture, mixing on low, and then add the rest of the flour mixture. Mix until just combined. Use a spatula to scrape down the sides and bottom of the bowl to ensure no pockets of flour are hiding. The batter can be baked as is, or with add-ins from the three versions below.

For version 1, in a small bowl, stir together the sugar and cinnamon. Add half of the batter to the loaf pan, sprinkle with 3 tablespoons (24 g) of the cinnamon-sugar mixture, and then add the remaining batter. Sprinkle with remaining cinnamon sugar.

For version 2, stir in the chocolate chips before pouring the batter into the loaf pan.

For version 3, stir in the craisins and chopped pecans before pouring the batter into the loaf pan.

Bake the loaf for 55 to 65 minutes, or until an inserted toothpick comes out with just a few moist crumbs. Cool for 10 to 15 minutes, and then carefully remove the loaf from the pan and cool on a cooling rack before serving. Keep in an airtight container for up to 1 week or freeze for up to 2 to 3 months.

Note: Baking time may vary depending on the thickness and/or darkness of your loaf pan.

squash snickerdoodle sandwich cookies with marshmallow filling

Did you know that, technically, all store-bought canned pumpkin puree is actually made from squash? There are a lot of intricacies involved in determining what's a squash versus a pumpkin (and how all pumpkins are actually a type of squash, but not all squash are pumpkins . . . are you confused yet?!), but the point of the story is, don't be afraid to use regular squash for baking! They have sweet, smooth textures (don't use a spaghetti squash, though) and are often seen around markets a little longer than pumpkins. These snickerdoodles can be made with either type of puree. I used a Tetsukabuto squash for mine, which has an incredible sweet, nutty flavor and the loveliest texture. Whatever puree you use, try and press out as much moisture as you can through a fine-mesh sieve, as a higher water content will result in a more cake-like cookie! The classic snickerdoodle tang and cinnamon sugar outside works so well with the squash. Make them into sandwich cookies by whipping up a marshmallow frosting, and toast the filling if you have a kitchen torch for an extra touch!

Yield: 24 cookies

COOKIES

3 cups (375 g) all-purpose flour

2 tsp (9 g) cream of tartar

1 tsp baking soda

¼ tsp salt

½ tsp ground allspice

1 cup (227 g) unsalted butter, room temperature

1⅓ cups (266 g) granulated sugar

1 large egg

½ cup (123 g) squash or pumpkin puree

1 tsp vanilla extract

CINNAMON-SUGAR TOPPING

½ cup (100 g) granulated sugar

½ tbsp (4 g) ground cinnamon

Preheat the oven to 350°F (180°C). Line two cookie sheets with parchment paper or silicone baking mats and set aside.

To make the cookies, in a medium bowl, combine the flour, cream of tartar, baking soda, salt and allspice and set aside. In the bowl of a stand mixer fitted with the paddle attachment, cream the butter and sugar for 2 minutes. Add the egg and mix well. Add the squash puree and vanilla and mix on low. Slowly add the dry ingredients. Scrape the sides of the bowl to ensure all the flour gets mixed in and beat on medium until just combined. Cover and refrigerate for about 30 minutes, or until the dough can easily be rolled into balls.

To make the cinnamon-sugar topping, in a medium bowl, mix together the sugar and cinnamon.

Use a cookie scoop to create equal-size dough balls and roll each one in the cinnamon-sugar mixture. Place the cookies onto the cookie sheets, a few inches (5 to 7.5 cm) apart. Use a firm flipper to press the cookies down a bit so they have a flat top and spread a bit. Bake for 10 to 12 minutes. Remove from the oven and let them cool for 10 minutes before transferring to a cooling rack. Repeat until the cookie dough is used up.

(continued)

MARSHMALLOW FILLING
(OPTIONAL)

½ cup (120 ml) egg whites
(about 4 large eggs)

1 cup (200 g) granulated sugar

⅛ tsp cream of tartar

¼ tsp salt

1 tsp vanilla extract

If making these into sandwich cookies, assemble them right before serving for best results. In a small saucepan, whisk together the egg whites and sugar. Assemble a double boiler by bringing a large pot of water containing a couple inches of water to a boil, and place the saucepan on top. Make sure the bottom doesn't touch the water. Stir occasionally, and heat until the mixture reaches 160°F (71°C) and stay there for a couple of minutes. Since we aren't cooking the marshmallow filling after it's made, this process is ensuring the eggs are safe to eat but can be skipped if using pasteurized eggs. Remove from the heat and place the mixture into the bowl of a stand mixer fitted with the whisk attachment. Add the cream of tartar and salt. Beat on medium-low for 4 minutes while the egg mixture cools, and then increase the speed to high for 4 minutes, or until it forms a thick and glossy meringue. Mix in the vanilla extract. Use immediately.

To assemble the sandwich cookies, place the marshmallow filling into a large piping bag fitted with a large open star tip. Pipe a generous amount of marshmallow filling onto the bottom of one cookie, use a kitchen torch to brown the marshmallow, if desired, and then place another cookie on top to finish the sandwich. Repeat for all of the cookies. Keep the cookies in an airtight container for a few days at room temperature or freeze them.

let it snow

Winter is a time to slow down, catch up on rest and paperwork and plan for the new year ahead. The farm is at its quietest, with all of the crops harvested and the trees bare, and perhaps there's a dusting of snow on the ground. On a rare occasion, we'll get hit with an ice storm. The orchard is especially striking when coated in ice. Eerie and ethereal. The trees look like they're made of glass, and each blade of grass crunches under your boots. Most fields lie empty and untouched until spring. The orchard, however, gets its annual pruning. We shape each tree by hand, increasing light, airflow and fruit production, while removing any disease we see. Many hours are spent in the quiet with just the trees for company, but it's always quite peaceful.

Winter is a season where I lean more heavily on nuts and spices, caramel and chocolate and a few jammy sweets, too. Breads seem to become the star of the show, and their time-consuming process doesn't seem so daunting when the weather makes you want to stay warm and toasty inside. Our apples store for months in our cold storage and may last into winter if we are lucky. That goes for pears as well, and then the grocery stores are flooded with citrus of all kinds. Lemons, limes, grapefruit and so many types of oranges. They may be available almost all year round, but, unsurprisingly, they do seem to shine during their peak season in winter.

This time of year is full of a lot of traditions, especially surrounding the abundance of parties, gatherings and holidays. Every year on Christmas Eve, I make a yule log icebox cake, coming up with a new flavor each year. I included my chestnut one for you to try (page 150). My Gingerbread Loaf with Chai-Spiced Poached Pears (page 155) is eye-catching and delicious, while the Cranberry-Coconut Granola (page 164) is the perfect snack for a road trip. Bring some brightness to your life with the Grapefruit-Lime-Chili Tart (page 175), which strikes an unusual balance with its sweet tart filling, chili-lime whipped cream and slightly savory thyme shortbread crust. I hope you find some new traditions on the following pages!

chestnut yule log icebox cake

It's a tradition that I bring a yule log icebox cake to Christmas dinner every year. It started way back when Joy the Baker shared her peppermint version, and I've been experimenting with different flavors ever since! Dairy free? Simply replace the whipped cream with whipped coconut cream. Easy peasy. This version features a chestnut cream, which feels so perfectly festive. Find boiled chestnuts in the international food aisle with other snacks, or you can substitute premade puree in a pinch. Cute little meringue mushrooms put the final magical touch on this simple dessert! Preparation is simple, but it does take several hours of freezing time before it's ready. I like making it over two days. It freezes extremely well, so it can be made days or weeks ahead of time, which can be helpful during a busy holiday season.

Yield: 6 servings

CHESTNUT PUREE

1 cup (240 ml) water

2 cups (260 g) boiled chestnuts

¼ cup (50 g) granulated sugar

1 tsp vanilla extract

CAKE

1½ cups (360 ml) whipping cream

2 tbsp (11 g) cocoa powder

1 tbsp (8 g) powdered sugar, or to taste, plus more for dusting

½ cup (120 ml) chestnut puree (see above)

30 thin chocolate wafers, such as Nabisco

To make the chestnut puree, place the water and boiled chestnuts into a food processor (or use a high-powered immersion blender) to blend until smooth. If using uncooked, shelled chestnuts, they will need to be boiled until soft before this step. Transfer the blended mixture to a medium saucepan and add the sugar. Bring to a simmer over medium heat and cook until the volume has reduced by about half. Stir constantly and be careful of the bubbling mixture! Remove from the heat, stir in the vanilla extract and chill the puree in the fridge before using.

To make the cake, in the bowl of a stand mixer fitted with the whisk attachment, whip the whipping cream on high for 2 to 4 minutes, or until medium peaks form. Add the cocoa powder, powdered sugar and the chestnut puree and gently fold together with a spatula. Mix for 1 to 2 minutes with the stand mixer if necessary to bring the mixture together. Add another tablespoon (8 g) of powdered sugar if you prefer a sweeter dessert.

Place about 1 tablespoon (15 g) of the chestnut whipped cream onto a thin chocolate cookie.

Repeat, and start stacking the cookies on top of each other.

Once you have 4 or 5 cookies stacked, gently flip the stack so they are now horizontal. These will form the log as you continue going.

Assemble the log in an airtight container that is at least over 14 inches (36 cm) long, as this will make transferring the dessert to the freezer much easier. Continue this process until all the cookies are used.

(continued)

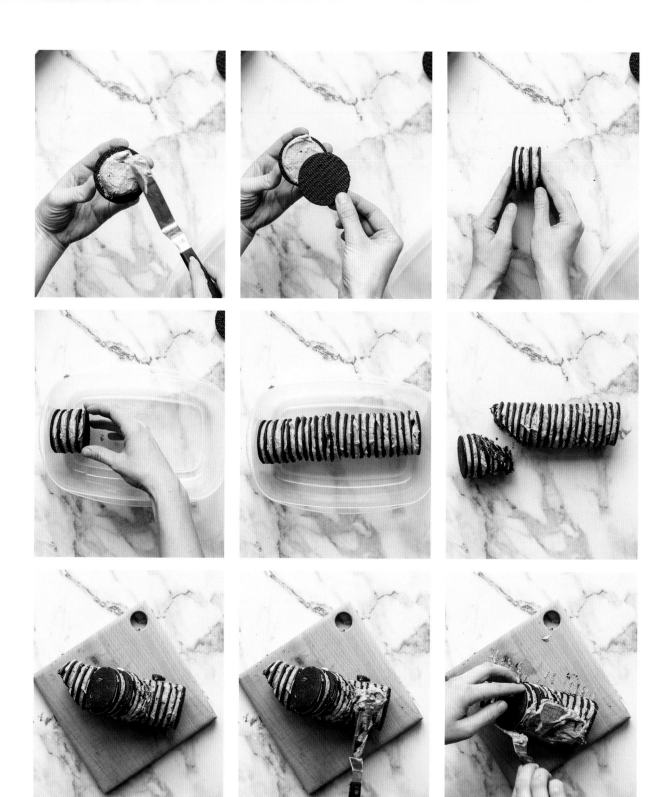

chestnut yule log icebox cake (continued)

MERINGUE MUSHROOMS

4 large egg whites

⅛ tsp cream of tartar

¼ tsp salt

1 cup (200 g) granulated sugar

1 tsp vanilla extract

2 tsp (10 ml) lemon juice

½ tbsp (4 g) cornstarch

¼ cup (44 g) chocolate chips

1 tbsp (5 g) cocoa powder

Note: Be sure to cut the log on a sharp diagonal angle when serving, so the distinctive stripes of the layers are on display.

The final log should be around 12 to 13 inches (30 to 33 cm) long. Transfer the log to the freezer and chill for about 1 hour, or until it's firm enough to handle without it sliding apart. Meanwhile, transfer the leftover whipped cream to the fridge. You should have about one-third of the whipped cream mixture left over.

While the log is freezing, make the mushroom meringues. Preheat the oven to 300°F (150°C). Line a large baking sheet with parchment paper and set aside.

In the bowl of a stand mixer fitted with the whisk attachment, whisk the egg whites with the cream of tartar and salt on medium until soft peaks form, about 2 to 3 minutes. Add the sugar 1 tablespoon (15 g) at a time, beating well after each addition. Repeat until all the sugar is incorporated and the meringue forms stiff and shiny peaks, about 8 minutes. Don't rush adding the sugar, as adding too much sugar at once can cause the meringue to deflate. Mix in the vanilla extract, lemon juice and cornstarch.

Transfer the meringue mixture to a large piping bag fitted with a small round tip. Pipe circles of varying sizes for the mushroom caps onto the parchment paper. Leave at least ½ inch (1.3 cm) between each meringue. Pipe mushroom stems by slowly drawing the piping bag straight up while applying firm pressure the entire time to pipe a tall meringue. You can always practice on a scrap of parchment paper and scrape the meringue back into the piping bag if they don't work out. Practice makes perfect.

Place the baking sheet in the oven and turn the temperature down to 250°F (120°C). Bake for 1 hour, or until the meringue is a very light cream color. Turn off the oven, leave the door cracked open and allow to cool completely inside the oven, at least 1 hour. The meringue can be stored in an airtight container in a cool, dry place for a couple of days before serving. They also freeze very well and only need a few minutes to thaw.

To assemble the mushrooms, melt the chocolate chips in a small bowl in the microwave, stirring every 10 seconds. Use a paring knife to cut a small hole in the bottom of the meringue mushroom caps. Dip the top of a meringue stem into the melted chocolate, and then place the prepared cap on top, fitting the stem into the small hole you cut. The chocolate will harden and stabilize the mushroom. Repeat for all the meringue, matching the sizes of stems and caps for different-size mushrooms. Use a pastry brush to dust the mushrooms with a bit of cocoa powder to look like dirt.

(continued)

chestnut yule log icebox cake (continued)

Remove the frozen cookie log from the freezer and carefully cut off a few inches from one end, cutting on a sharp diagonal.

This small piece will become the branch of the yule log. Now is a good time to move the log to its serving dish if possible. Use a tablespoon (15 g) of whipped cream to attach the branch you just cut to the top of the cookie log or to the side for a more stable dessert.

Cover the entire cookie log with the remaining whipped cream.

Use a butter knife or offset spatula to drag lines across the log to mimic bark.

Use a skewer or fork to create tree rings on the ends. If you have a large enough airtight container, move the entire dessert and serving tray into it. Otherwise, transfer the serving dish with the dessert back to the freezer for about 1 hour, or until solid, and then wrap in plastic wrap. Store the cake until ready to serve. It will keep for several months and is great to make ahead of time.

Remove the dessert from the freezer for 15 to 20 minutes to thaw on the counter or transfer to the fridge a few hours before serving. The dessert should still be cold and the whipped cream not sloppy, but it shouldn't be frozen in the middle. The cookies will now have a cake-like consistency. Decorate the log with mushroom meringues and dust with powdered sugar at the table while serving. Store any leftovers in the freezer for up to 2 months.

gingerbread loaf with chai-spiced poached pears

Similar to apples, pears will keep for several months into winter when stored in a cold place. Our large walk-in cooler is kept at 1°C (about 34°F), which makes for chilly working conditions, but it keeps our produce happy! Pears are a wonderful vessel for winter desserts, as their mellow flavor pairs well with cozy spices. Poach them with ginger, cloves and a cinnamon stick for maximum flavor. The pears will then be nestled into a decadent batter made with fresh ginger and molasses for a loaf full of warmth. Use small pears here so that the loaf pan doesn't get too full! Cutting into this loaf is incredibly satisfying, as the pears truly steal the show.

Yield: 1 (5 x 9–inch [13 x 23–cm]) loaf

POACHED PEARS

4 cups (960 ml) water, plus extra if needed

1 cup (200 g) granulated sugar

3 small pears, peeled (I used Bosc)

1" (2.5-cm) piece of ginger, minced

1 cinnamon stick

1 tsp whole cloves

To make the poached pears, in a large saucepan, place the water and sugar and bring to a gentle boil.

Add the pears, ginger, cinnamon stick and cloves. If any of the pears are sticking out of the water, place a circle of parchment on top of the pears with the center cut out of it to create a donut shape. This will keep the pears submerged while letting the steam out. Add more water if necessary to completely the cover pears. Reduce the heat to medium-low and cook for 25 to 30 minutes, or until the pears are easily pierced with a fork. Remove from the heat and let the pears cool in their liquid. Store in an airtight container in their liquid in the fridge, and they will continue to soak up the flavor. Poached pears will keep for about 5 days in the fridge.

Preheat the oven to 350°F (180°C). Grease and line a 5 x 9–inch (13 x 23–cm) loaf pan with parchment paper and set aside.

Note: You may choose to use a small paring knife to carve a small circle into the bottom and up the middle of the pears to remove seeds, if desired. However, this isn't necessary, as you can remove the seeds from the loaf once the pieces are sliced, and the loaf will cook better without the batter entering the pears.

(continued)

GINGERBREAD LOAF

½ cup (114 g) unsalted butter, room temperature

½ cup (100 g) granulated sugar

2 large eggs

⅓ cup (80 ml) cooking molasses (not blackstrap)

1 tbsp (15 ml) vanilla extract

2 tbsp (6 g) freshly minced ginger or 1½ tsp (3 g) ground ginger

½ tsp ground cinnamon

½ tsp ground allspice

½ tsp salt

1½ tsp (7 g) baking powder

½ tsp baking soda

2 cups (250 g) all-purpose flour

¾ cup (180 ml) plain Greek yogurt

To make the gingerbread loaf, in the bowl of a stand mixer fitted with the paddle attachment, mix together the butter and sugar on medium-high for 2 to 3 minutes, or until light and fluffy. Add the eggs one at a time and mix on medium until each one is incorporated. Add the molasses, vanilla extract and ginger and mix on medium until well mixed. Use a spatula to scrape down the sides and bottom of the bowl. In a medium bowl, whisk together the cinnamon, allspice, salt, baking powder, baking soda and flour. Add half of this mixture to the wet ingredients and mix on low until almost combined. Then add the yogurt, mixing on low until nearly combined, and then finish with the remaining dry ingredients. Try not to mix more than you have to. The batter will be quite thick, and that's normal.

Scoop about one-third of the batter into the prepared pan. Then nestle the pears into the batter and spoon the remaining batter around the pears. The pan should be no more than three-quarters full, so if your pears were large, you may have leftover batter. Do not overfill the loaf pan, but rather bake any remaining batter in a small loaf pan or muffin tin until an inserted toothpick comes out clean. Bake the loaf for 50 to 60 minutes, or until an inserted tooth-pick comes out clean (avoid poking it into the pears). Let the loaf cool in the pan for 5 to 10 minutes, and then carefully remove using the parchment paper and cool further. This is best served the first day.

Note: Small pears work best for this recipe, as large pears can over-crowd the loaf pan and not bake as well. Also, poaching the pears adds flavor and sweetness, but this step can be skipped if you're short on time. Pears can also be left out, and you'll still have a deliciously cozy gingerbread loaf.

sour cream–cardamom cake donuts

When I was a child, my grandpa worked on our farm five days a week, which meant that when my sister and I got home from school, he'd often be sitting in the kitchen with our dad enjoying a coffee break. This was my normal, and I realize now how special it is that we had so much time together. Our coffee break snacks were usually fresh cookies, brownies and sometimes pie! All delicious. But if I had to choose, I'd pick donuts as the perfect coffee break treat. These old-fashioned sour cream donuts are a go-to of mine. They get an extra boost of flavor from the spelt flour and are covered in a cozy cardamom glaze to finish them off. They're made with baking powder, not yeast, so they're nice and quick to whip up.

Yield: 10–12 donuts

DONUTS

¼ cup (57 g) unsalted butter, room temperature

½ cup (100 g) granulated sugar

1 large egg

½ cup (120 ml) full-fat sour cream

1 cup (125 g) all-purpose flour

1 cup (125 g) spelt flour

½ tsp salt

1½ tsp baking powder

¼ tsp ground cardamom

Neutral oil, for frying (I like canola), amount will vary depending on fry method

To make the donuts, in the bowl of a stand mixer fitted with the paddle attachment, cream together the butter and sugar on medium-high for 2 to 3 minutes. Reduce to low and add the egg. Mix until well combined. Add the sour cream and mix together on low. Be sure to scrape down the sides and bottom of the bowl with a spatula to ensure everything is evenly combined. In a separate bowl, whisk together the all-purpose flour, spelt flour, salt, baking powder and ground cardamom. With the mixer on low, slowly add the flour mixture to the wet and mix until almost combined. Remove the bowl from the stand mixer and use a spatula to finish mixing the dough together. The dough will be sticky, and that's just right! Cover the bowl with plastic wrap and transfer to the fridge for about 1 hour, or until you can roll it out easily.

Line a large baking sheet with parchment paper. When the dough is chilled, roll it out onto a lightly floured surface to ½ inch (1.3 cm) thick. Use a donut cutter or two round circle cutters (one large and one small) to cut the donut shapes. Place donuts onto the parchment-lined baking sheet as you work. Gently press together any leftover dough scraps, roll them out again and cut more donuts. When all the dough is used up, place the baking sheet into the fridge to chill.

In a deep fryer, an electric skillet or a large, heavy bottomed pan, heat the oil to 375°F (190°C). There should be enough oil that your donut will float about 2 inches (5 cm) above the bottom, while being about half immersed. Line a wire cooling rack with a few sheets of paper towel to absorb the oil, place the rack over a large baking sheet (this will catch any large oil drips) and move it beside the fryer. If you aren't using a deep fryer with a basket, then a spider strainer works perfectly for dropping the doughnuts into the oil as well as removing them.

(continued)

sour cream–cardamom cake donuts (continued)

1 cup (120 g) powdered sugar, plus extra if needed

2 tbsp (30 ml) milk, plus extra if needed

½ tsp vanilla extract

¼ tsp ground cardamom, or to taste

Note: A deep fryer works best, although I've used an electric frying pan for many years as well. These both control the temperature for you, and I find them safer to use compared to a pot on the stove. If you use a pot on the stove, make sure it's a heavy-bottomed one, which will absorb and distribute heat more evenly and help keep the temperature steady. You will need a candy/deep fryer thermometer on hand to keep an eye on the temperature.

Once your oil is up to temperature, remove the donuts from the fridge and fry 2 or 3 at a time, being careful not to crowd them. They should initially sink to the bottom of the fryer and then float for the majority of the cook time. Always try frying a test donut first. Allow the test donut to cool slightly, and then cut it open to check its doneness. If your oil is too hot, the donut may get too dark but be undercooked inside; but if it's not hot enough, it will take too long to cook and you'll end up with an oily donut. Fry the donuts for about 2 minutes per side, or until golden brown. Remove from the oil and place onto the paper towel–lined cooling rack. Repeat with all the donuts.

While the donuts are cooling, make the glaze. In a medium bowl, whisk together the powdered sugar, milk, vanilla extract and cardamom. Add more milk or powdered sugar if necessary until the desired consistency is reached. Place a wire cooling rack over a baking sheet to catch the excess glaze, and dip each donut in the glaze and place onto the rack. The glaze will set in 5 to 10 minutes, and they'll be ready to serve. As with all donuts, these are best served immediately or at least the same day.

chocolate cheesecake with cranberry sauce, sugared rosemary and cranberries

Winter is a time for decadence, and this cheesecake fits the bill perfectly. Chocolate cheesecake, a chocolate crust and a tart cranberry sauce to go on top. The sugared rosemary and cranberry garnishes help make things festive. Sugaring treats is so easy, and it tempers the zip of the fresh cranberries while adding a touch of elegance to a simple dessert. Rich, decadent and simple to put together, this dessert keeps well and is a great choice to make ahead of time.

Yield: 1 (9-inch [23-cm]) cheesecake

CRUST

1⅓ cups (133 g) chocolate baking crumbs, such as Oreo Baking Crumbs

6 tbsp (90 ml) melted unsalted butter

Pinch of salt

CHEESECAKE

1½ cups (225 g) chopped semi or bittersweet chocolate

1¼ cups (300 ml) whipping cream

2 cups (464 g) full-fat cream cheese, room temperature (2 packages)

¼ cup (22 g) cocoa powder (use half black cocoa powder if you have it)

½ cup (60 g) powdered sugar

CRANBERRY SAUCE

½ cup (120 ml) water

⅓ cup (66 g) granulated sugar

2 cups (200 g) cranberries

To make the crust, in a medium bowl, stir together the chocolate baking crumbs, melted butter and salt and firmly press into the bottom of a 9-inch (23-cm) springform pan. Transfer to the fridge to set.

To make the cheesecake, melt the chocolate using a double boiler (see page 71) or warm up in the microwave, being sure to stir every 10 seconds. Set aside to cool slightly. In the bowl of a stand mixer fitted with the whisk attachment, whip the whipping cream on high until soft peaks form, about 2 to 3 minutes. Spoon into a separate bowl and set aside. Use the same stand mixer bowl (no need to clean it) and fit the mixer with the paddle attachment. Mix the cream cheese on medium for 1 to 2 minutes, until smooth and creamy. Sift the cocoa powder and powdered sugar together and add to the cream cheese. Mix on low for 1 to 2 minutes, until fully incorporated. Use a spatula to scrape down the sides and bottom of the bowl. With the mixer on low, slowly stream in the melted chocolate and mix until smooth. Carefully fold about one-third of the whipped cream into the cream cheese mixture until almost combined. Then add the remaining whipped cream and carefully fold in until completely combined. Pour the mixture into the prepared crust and refrigerate for 3 to 4 hours or overnight.

To make the cranberry sauce, in a medium saucepan, combine the water and sugar and bring to a boil over medium-high heat. Add the cranberries and cook until they pop and start to break down. For a perfectly smooth sauce, remove from the heat, and puree using a high-speed blender or immersion blender and strain through a fine-mesh sieve. Return to the heat and cook until the sauce thickens slightly. Cool to room temperature and transfer to an airtight container in the fridge until ready to assemble the cheesecake.

Line a large rimmed baking sheet with parchment paper and set aside.

(continued)

chocolate cheesecake with cranberry sauce, sugared rosemary and cranberries (continued)

SUGARED ROSEMARY AND CRANBERRIES

1 cup (240 ml) water

½ cup (100 g) granulated sugar, plus more as needed

1 cup (100 g) cranberries

Fresh rosemary sprigs, as desired

To make the sugared cranberries and rosemary, in a small saucepan, bring the water and sugar to a boil and boil for 3 minutes. Remove from the heat and add the cranberries. Immediately scoop the cranberries out, strain and transfer to the prepared pan. Dip sprigs of rosemary into the sugar water, shake off excess water and move to the pan. If any cranberries or rosemary appear to be sitting in a pool of water, simply move them to a new spot. We want them sticky but not dripping with the sugar water. Let everything dry slightly for 15 to 20 minutes. Meanwhile, place sugar into a pie dish or shallow bowl. Add the cranberries to the sugar and shake to cover completely. Repeat with the rosemary. Use immediately or store in an airtight container in the fridge. They may weep slightly when stored. If so, simply toss them in more sugar to perk them up.

To assemble the cheesecake, spread the cranberry sauce over the cheesecake or reserve for each person to drizzle over their own. Garnish with the sugared cranberries and rosemary and serve. Store leftovers in an airtight container for up to 1 week. If left on the cheesecake, the rosemary will infuse its flavor over time.

Note: Black cocoa powder is heavily Dutched and is strong in flavor. I like the flavor and color it brings to this recipe, but it won't make a huge difference if you simply use regular cocoa powder.

cranberry-coconut granola

Pruning our apple trees is the biggest job we have to get done in winter. We wait until all the leaves fall off so that we can see the branches, and then we cut, cut, cut. This increases light availability, airflow and fruit production! It also is a great tool for managing and removing disease. Most years it will snow a few times, and the white backdrop actually makes it easier to see the shape of the branches. The soft sound of your boots crunching in the snow and the snip of your pruners break the silence of the orchard. Crunchy granola is always a great snack to carry along in your pockets. I love adding dried cranberries and coconut flakes in winter, and I will mix it up as the seasons change. Puffed quinoa adds a unique texture and can often be found in a mix with puffed sorghum and black bean crisps. Black beans may be an odd ingredient in granola. While they don't add much flavor beyond a satisfying crunch in this crispy form, they do add a boost of fiber and protein. Feel free to adjust to your own taste and make it your own! Remember, the key to crunchy, chunky granola is letting it cool completely before breaking it up!

Yield: 1 (10 x 15–inch [25 x 38–cm]) pan of granola

2½ cups (225 g) rolled oats

1 cup (70 g) puffed quinoa, or a combination of puffed quinoa, sorghum and black bean crisps

¾ cup (82 g) chopped pecans

½ cup (54 g) slivered almonds

½ cup (47 g) large flaked unsweetened coconut

¼ cup (30 g) pumpkin seeds (pepitas)

½ cup (73 g) craisins

1 tsp salt

½ tsp cinnamon

½ cup (110 g) coconut oil

½ cup (120 ml) liquid honey

1 tsp vanilla extract

Preheat the oven to 350°F (180°C). Line a 10 x 15–inch (25 x 38–cm) rimmed jelly roll pan with parchment paper and set aside.

In a large bowl, stir together the rolled oats, puffed quinoa, pecans, almonds, coconut, pumpkin seeds, craisins, salt and cinnamon. Set aside. In a small saucepan over low heat, melt together the coconut oil and honey, stirring until combined. Remove from the heat and stir in the vanilla extract. Pour over the oat mixture and stir until completely mixed. Dump the granola onto the prepared pan and press firmly into an even layer. Bake for 10 to 12 minutes, and then rotate the pan, stir the granola and press firmly back into the pan. Bake for 10 to 12 minutes, or until the granola is a light golden brown. Be careful not to burn it! Remove from the oven and allow to cool completely before breaking it up and storing it. (I know this is hard to do . . . but trust me!) This helps maximize the amount of large crunchy chunks that form. Store in an airtight container for up to 1 week.

Note: Our local bulk food retailer always carries a mix of puffed quinoa, puffed sorghum and black bean crisps.

chocolate chunk spelt cookies with rosemary and flaked sea salt

Even in the dead of winter when the fields are bare and the orchard is a barren brown, our rosemary bushes stand out as a beacon of hope. Hardy, fragrant and green, they help carry us through the colder months, allowing us to harvest a wee bit of something fresh. Perfect for adding to biscuits, breads and, dare I say, . . . cookies. I adore the slightly savory, unexpected flavor it brings to a classic chocolate chip cookie. If that freaks you out, feel free to leave the rosemary out, and you'll still have a darn good cookie.

Yield: 2 dozen cookies (depending on the size of cookie scoop)

1 cup (227 g) salted butter, room temperature

1 cup (220 g) packed brown sugar

½ cup (100 g) granulated sugar

1 large egg

2 tsp (10 ml) vanilla extract

1 tsp baking soda

1 tbsp (2 g) finely chopped fresh rosemary

1¼ cups (156 g) all-purpose flour

1¼ cups (156 g) spelt flour

1 cup (175 g) semisweet chocolate chips or chunks of chopped chocolate (I often do a few chunks of bittersweet Belgian chocolate pressed into the top of the cookie.)

Flaked salt, as desired

Preheat the oven to 350°F (180°C). Line a 10 x 15–inch (25 x 38–cm) baking sheet with parchment paper or a silicone baking mat and set aside.

In the bowl of a stand mixer fitted with the paddle attachment, cream the butter, brown sugar and granulated sugar on medium for 3 to 5 minutes, until it has lightened in color and is quite fluffy. Add the egg and mix on medium until fully incorporated. Add the vanilla, baking soda and rosemary and mix on low until incorporated. Mix in the flours on low until the dough just comes together. Use a spatula to scrape down the sides and bottom of the bowl. Stir in the chocolate while mixing on low or simply fold in by hand with a spatula. Use a cookie scoop or a spoon to form balls of cookie dough and place onto the prepared baking sheet. Bake for 9 to 11 minutes, making sure the centers aren't quite set. Remove from the oven and immediately sprinkle with flaked salt so that it will stick to the cookies, and cool slightly before serving. Cookies will store in an airtight container for 1 week or so. Freeze in an airtight container for longer.

cookie tips

I always recommend doing one or two test cookies first in order to figure out your exact desired cookie consistency. Bake time will vary depending on the color and thickness of your cookie sheet, as well as your oven. I prefer for my cookies to almost look underbaked when you remove them from the oven, to ensure that the middle is nice and soft.

Are your cookies too flat for your preference? Pop them in the freezer for a 5- to 10-minute chill, or try adding ¼ cup (31 g) more of flour. This is why test cookies are important!

Freeze unbaked cookie balls individually on a baking sheet and move to an airtight container once frozen, because sometimes you just want to bake one cookie! Bake from frozen and increase bake time by 1 minute.

lemon curd ice cream

Ice storms occur on our farm every so often. Freezing raindrops turn our leafless orchard into the most wondrous sight as every branch, blade of grass and odd forgotten apple is encased in a glassy cage. Ethereal is the perfect word to describe it. My preferred form of ice in winter, however, is ice cream. I'm a firm believer that ice cream belongs in all seasons, and I love using citrus to add a little brightness to a season that can get a little depressing. Zingy and bursting with flavor, the lemon curd balances so well with the creamy, rich, custard base of the ice cream to bring you the perfect dessert for a dreary winter day.

Yield: about 5 cups (680 g) of ice cream

2 cups (480 ml) whole milk

2 cups (480 ml) heavy whipping cream

8 large egg yolks

¾ cup (150 g) granulated sugar

1 tbsp (6 g) lemon zest (about 1 lemon)

1 tsp vanilla extract

½ cup (120 ml) Lemon Curd (page 208), plus extra for optional topping

In a medium saucepan, whisk together the milk, cream, egg yolks, sugar, lemon zest and vanilla. Heat on medium-high, whisking continuously. Bring the mixture to 170°F (77°C) as this ensures your yolks are safe to eat, or until you dip a spoon into the mixture and can run your finger through the custard without it running, about 10 minutes. Cool the mixture by setting the saucepan into a bath of ice water and stirring occasionally to release the heat.

Once the mixture has reached room temperature, you can cool further in the fridge for 2 to 3 hours, or place directly into your ice cream maker and follow your machine's instructions. My maker takes about 20 to 30 minutes, and the texture gets quite thick. Layer one-half of the ice cream into a container, drizzle about ¼ cup (60 ml) of lemon curd into the ice cream and run a knife through to swirl. Repeat with the remaining ice cream and curd. Serve immediately as soft serve or place into an airtight container and store in the freezer. You can serve with additional lemon curd on top, if you wish.

Note: A quick-read thermometer can be helpful when making the custard base, but is not necessary.

orange-chocolate swirl bread with maple–cream cheese glaze

Chocolate and orange are always a good pairing. Rich sweetness combined with the bright zesty citrus notes make this bread sing with flavor. Now, I know that the swirl is one of those things that looks mighty impressive and complicated, but really, it isn't actually that hard! The approach is similar to making cinnamon buns, but once you roll the filling up into the dough, you simply cut the rolled log in half and twist it together instead of cutting it into buns. See? Easy peasy. You can do it, I promise!

Yield: 1 (5 x 9–inch [13 x 23–cm]) loaf

DOUGH

½ cup (120 ml) whole milk

¼ cup (50 g) granulated sugar, divided

2¼ tsp (7 g) active dry yeast

¼ cup (57 g) unsalted butter

1 large egg

1 tsp vanilla extract

2 tbsp (12 g) orange zest (about 1 large orange)

½ tsp salt

2¼–2¾ cups (281–344 g) all-purpose flour

CHOCOLATE FILLING

½ cup (88 g) semisweet chocolate chips

¼ cup (57 g) unsalted butter, room temperature

¼ cup (50 g) granulated sugar

¼ cup (22 g) cocoa powder

To make the dough, in a small saucepan, heat the milk and 1 teaspoon of the granulated sugar on medium until the mixture starts to steam. Remove from the heat and stir in the yeast. Set aside to rise. If the mixture is not frothy within 5 to 10 minutes, discard and try again. Or you may need fresher yeast. In the bowl of a stand mixer fitted with the paddle attachment, stir together the remaining granulated sugar, butter, egg, vanilla, orange zest, salt and 1 cup (125 g) of the flour on medium. Add the yeast mixture when frothy and continue to mix on medium until the dough starts to come together. Switch from the paddle attachment to the dough hook, and add 1 more cup (125 g) of flour. Mix on low and add more flour by the tablespoon (8 g) until the dough comes away from the sides of the bowl and forms a ball. Continue to mix on low for 8 to 10 minutes. If the dough ever starts to stick, add another tablespoon (8 g) of flour. The dough should stay tacky, so add as little flour as you can. Remove from the bowl and knead for 2 to 3 minutes by hand on a clean counter. Transfer into a large greased bowl, cover with a clean dish towel and place in a warm spot to rise until doubled, about 1 hour.

While the dough is rising, make the chocolate filling. Melt the chocolate using a double boiler (see page 71) or warm up in the microwave, being sure to stir every 10 seconds. Set aside to cool slightly. In a medium bowl, stir together the butter, sugar, melted chocolate and cocoa powder until smooth. Allow to cool to room temperature before using, otherwise it will run out of the dough and create a big mess. If it seems too runny, place it in the fridge for 5-minute intervals and stir well in between each time until it firms up a little.

Grease a 5 x 9–inch (13 x 23–cm) loaf pan and set aside.

(continued)

1 large egg, lightly beaten

GLAZE

2 tbsp (30 g) cream cheese, softened

1 tbsp (15 ml) maple syrup, or more as needed

½ cup (60 g) powdered sugar, or more as needed

To make the bread, roll the dough into a rectangle about 10 x 15 inches (25 x 38 cm). Spread the chocolate mixture evenly over the dough, and then roll the dough up tightly. Start with the long edge facing you and roll toward the other long edge. Pinch the seam shut tightly and turn the log so the seam is underneath. Trim each end so they're straight. Use a sharp serrated knife to cut the log lengthwise down the center, creating two long halves. Gently turn each log so that the layers of chocolate are facing up. Pinch together the dough ends at one end, and then twist the dough around itself. Lift the right log up and over the left and repeat. Pinch the remaining end together. (See step-by-step photos at the end of the recipe for reference.) Carefully transfer the dough to the prepared pan, cover with a clean dish towel and let rise until puffy, about 30 minutes.

Preheat the oven to 350°F (180°C).

When the dough is ready, brush with the lightly beaten egg. Bake for 28 to 30 minutes, or until the top is deep golden brown. The chocolate filling will look black, and that's normal and doesn't mean it's burnt. Cool for 5 to 10 minutes before removing from the pan and cool further.

While the bread is baking, make the glaze. In a medium bowl, whisk together the cream cheese, maple syrup and powdered sugar. Add more syrup or powdered sugar as needed to adjust the consistency. Set aside until the bread is done.

Serve the bread slightly warm with a generous drizzle of the glaze. Store the bread in an airtight container for several days or slice and freeze for up to 3 months.

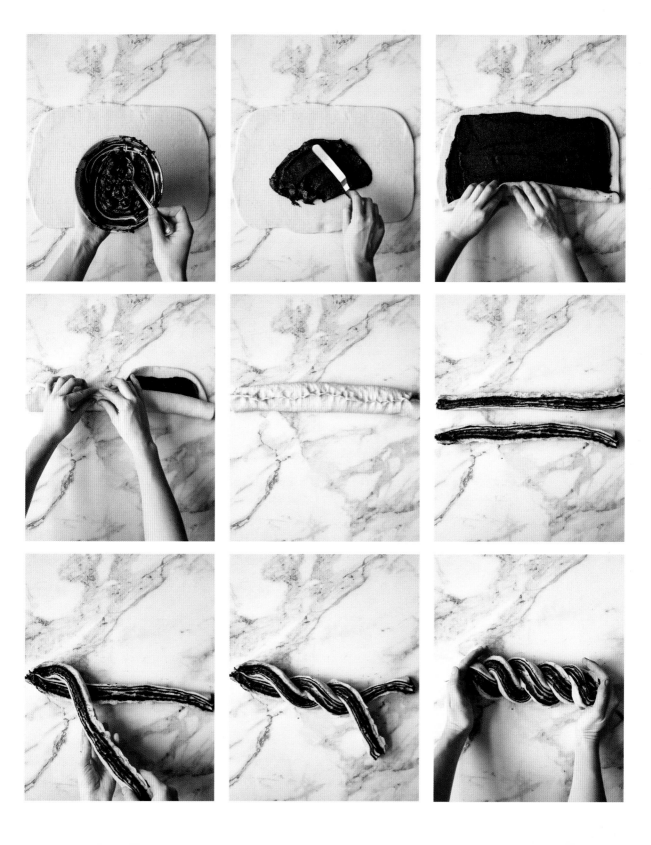

grapefruit-lime-chili tart with thyme shortbread crust

Winter months spent inside can make a person go a little stir-crazy. Baking is always something I turn to for comfort, and I am forever grateful that citrus season peaks during these months. Chili and lime just belong together, and the heat from the chili brings something amazing out of this tart. The grapefruit brings a tartness, which is tempered by the sugar in the creamy filling. Be brave and try it!

Yield: 1 (9-inch [23-cm]) tart

THYME SHORTBREAD CRUST

½ cup (114 g) unsalted butter, room temperature

1½ cups (188 g) all-purpose flour

⅓ cup (40 g) powdered sugar

⅛ tsp salt

1 tsp finely chopped fresh thyme

GRAPEFRUIT FILLING

2 tbsp (12 g) grapefruit zest (about 1 medium grapefruit)

¾ cup (150 g) granulated sugar

⅔ cup (160 ml) fresh-squeezed grapefruit juice

5 large eggs

½ cup (114 g) unsalted butter

WHIPPED CREAM

1 cup (240 ml) whipping cream

1 tbsp (8 g) powdered sugar

½ tsp vanilla extract

1 tsp lime zest (about ½ lime)

Chili powder, for garnishing

Preheat the oven to 350°F (180°C).

To make the crust, in the bowl of a stand mixer fitted with the paddle attachment, mix together the butter, flour, powdered sugar, salt and thyme until completely mixed and crumb-like. Pour the crumbs into a 9-inch (23-cm) tart pan with a removable bottom or a pie dish. Firmly press toward the edges first, creating an outer crust about ¼ inch (6 mm) thick. Make sure to press into the bottom edge very well, otherwise it will be thick and tough to get a fork through. Distribute the rest of the crumbs across the bottom of the pan and press down firmly. Pierce the bottom with a sharp knife to create several vent holes. Bake for 18 to 20 minutes, or until lightly brown. Remove and let cool while you prepare the filling.

To make the grapefruit filling, place a large fine-mesh sieve over a heatproof bowl and set aside. In a medium heavy-bottomed saucepan, massage the zest into the sugar until completely combined and fragrant. Add the grapefruit juice and eggs and whisk to combine. Cook on medium heat, whisking the entire time. Do not walk away or stop whisking, as the eggs can separate out and cook into a lumpy mess. Cook for 8 to 10 minutes, or until the mixture has thickened. It will look like pudding, and you should be able to run the whisk through and see the bottom of the pot before it settles again. It will thicken further as it cools. Remove from the heat and press through the prepared sieve to remove the grapefruit zest and any stray bits of egg that may have cooked separately. Whisk in the butter, a few tablespoons at a time, until completely combined. Pour the mixture into the tart crust and allow to cool to about room temperature before moving to an airtight container and transferring to the fridge. Chill for at least 3 hours or overnight before serving.

To make the whipped cream, in a stand mixer fitted with the whisk attachment, whip the cream on high until medium peaks form. Add the powdered sugar, vanilla extract and lime zest. Whip until just incorporated. Whipped cream is best if made right before serving, but it will keep in an airtight container in the fridge for a few days.

Serve the chilled tart with a dollop of lime whipped cream and a generous amount of chili powder. Store leftovers in the fridge for up to 3 days.

mocha cream puffs

There are few things farmers hate more than paperwork. We just want to be outside! Copious amounts of coffee are required in order for us to stay awake and attentive indoors. My favorite beans are from a local roaster, because (shocker!) buying local, freshly roasted beans is seriously a game changer. The mocha whipped cream in this recipe has the perfect balance of bittersweet deliciousness, while the chocolate ganache finishes off the cream puffs beautifully. They pair perfectly with (you guessed it!) a good cup of coffee!

Yield: 12–15 cream puffs

FOR THE CREAM PUFFS

¼ cup (57 g) unsalted butter, room temperature

¼ cup (60 ml) water

¼ cup (60 ml) whole milk

1 tsp granulated sugar

⅛ tsp salt

½ cup (63 g) all-purpose flour

2 large eggs, beaten

Preheat the oven to 400°F (200°C). Line a large rimmed baking sheet with a silicone mat or parchment paper. Prepare a piping bag fitted with a medium-size round tip. (Alternatively, the cream puffs may simply be spooned onto the baking sheet.)

To make the cream puffs, in a medium saucepan, combine the butter, water and milk on medium heat. Use a wooden spoon to stir the mixture and bring to a boil. Add the sugar, salt and flour, turn off the heat and stir constantly with the wooden spoon for 1 to 2 minutes, until the dough comes away from the sides of the pan and forms a ball. I like to press the dough up against the sides and bottom of the pan to help cook off the excess moisture. The batter is ready when a thin film forms on the bottom of the saucepan. Remove from the burner and place the dough into the bowl of a stand mixer fitted with the paddle attachment, and allow to cool for several minutes. Add half the beaten eggs, and on medium speed, mix until fully incorporated. The dough may look curdled at first, so just keep mixing. Slowly add the rest of the egg mixture, reserving 1 to 2 tablespoons (15 to 30 ml). Mix the dough for another minute and observe the texture. Dip a clean spoon into the batter and lift straight up and out. If the batter forms a nice "V" off the end of the spoon and is thick, shiny and pipeable, then it's ready. If the batter is too dry and thick and doesn't form a "V", then stream in the reserved egg mixture.

Fill your prepared piping bag with the batter and pipe your puffs onto the baking sheet. They should be about 2 inches (5 cm) in diameter, about ½ to 1 inch (1.3 to 2.5 cm) in height and 1½ inches (4 cm) apart. Use a wet fingertip to gently smooth down any peaks that form while piping, otherwise they may burn.

Bake for 10 minutes, and then reduce the heat to 350°F (180°C) and bake for an additional 20 to 25 minutes. You'll know they're done when they are puffed and the tops are golden brown. In the last few minutes of baking, I like to remove one from the oven and see if it deflates after a minute. If not, I cut it open to check the inside. It should be mostly hollow and not too gummy. But don't open the oven door during the first 25 minutes of baking! This can cause them to lose their lift and deflate. Remove from the oven, transfer to a cooling rack and allow to cool completely before filling.

(continued)

mocha cream puffs (continued)

MOCHA WHIPPED CREAM

2 cups (480 ml) whipping cream

1 tsp vanilla extract

¼ cup (22 g) cocoa powder

1 tbsp (5 g) espresso powder

3 tbsp (24 g) powdered sugar

CHOCOLATE GANACHE

½ cup (120 ml) whipping cream

½ cup (75 g) finely chopped good-quality semisweet chocolate

FOR SERVING (OPTIONAL)

Sprinkles, as desired

Powdered sugar, as desired

While the cream puffs cool, make the whipped cream. Prepare a piping bag with a large star tip and set aside. In the bowl of a stand mixer fitted with the whisk attachment, whip the whipping cream on high until it starts to thicken slightly. Add the vanilla, cocoa powder, espresso powder and powdered sugar. Whip until stiff peaks form. Transfer the whipped cream to the prepared piping bag.

To make the ganache, in a small saucepan, heat the whipping cream until it just starts to simmer, stirring every so often. Remove from the heat and add the finely chopped chocolate. Let it sit undisturbed for 1 to 2 minutes, and then use a wooden spoon or rubber spatula to gently mix it together. If the chocolate doesn't melt completely, simply place it back onto low heat and stir constantly until the mixture is completely smooth.

To assemble the cream puffs, cut each puff in half, spoon a tablespoon (15 g) of ganache into the bottom and then pipe whipped cream on top to fill. Carefully dip the top half of the cream puff into the ganache and place on top of the whipped cream filling. Add sprinkles and/or dust with powdered sugar, if desired. Serve immediately or keep in the fridge until ready to serve. Cream puffs may be frozen in an airtight container for longer storage, either unfilled or filled. Allow to thaw in the fridge before serving.

brown butter buckwheat tarts

Butter tarts are one of the most indulgent treats we make around the holidays, and they are a favorite of my dad's. A buttery, custardy filling goes into a tart shell along with nuts and raisins (or without raisins if you're on "team no raisin" like me!). This version features brown butter, maple syrup and a buckwheat crust for some added wholesomeness! Short on time? Pick up frozen premade tart shells to make your life a little easier. These tarts keep well in the freezer and are fantastic to pull out when company stops in.

Yield: 18–24 tarts

1 batch Pie Dough with buckwheat flour variation (page 191)

½ cup (114 g) unsalted butter

2 large eggs

½ cup (110 g) packed brown sugar

½ cup (120 ml) maple syrup

¼ cup (60 ml) whipping cream

¼ tsp salt

1 cup (145 g) raisins, presoaked for 10 minutes

½ cup (55 g) roughly chopped pecans or walnuts

1 tsp vanilla extract

Note: The pie crust will need to be prepared at least 1 hour before starting the pie but preferably the day before. The crust will keep in an airtight container in the fridge for 2 to 3 days or for up to 3 months in the freezer. (Thaw in the fridge before using.)

Set an ungreased muffin tin beside your workspace. Prepare the pie dough. Remove the disk of pie dough from the fridge and let it rest on the counter for about 15 minutes, or until you can roll it out without cracking. Just don't let it get too soft! Roll the dough out on a lightly floured surface. Use a round cookie cutter between 3 to 5 inches (8 to 13 cm) in diameter to cut out tart shells. A 3-inch (8-cm) cookie cutter will give you a smaller, more tart-like dessert and will only come up to about half the muffin tin height. Use a fluted cookie cutter for a fancier edge. Transfer each dough round to the muffin tin and press the dough in firmly. Repeat with all the dough. Transfer the muffin tin of tart shells to the fridge or freezer to chill for 5 to 10 minutes, or until the dough is firm. The exact timing may vary depending on dough thickness. Collect the dough scraps, gently press them together and repeat. If the dough gets too warm, place it back into the fridge until it is cold enough to roll out again.

Preheat the oven to 375°F (190°C).

While the tart shells are chilling, prepare the filling. In a medium saucepan, brown the butter over medium heat, stirring constantly. The butter will start to foam and will then start browning. It's ready when you can see brown flecks under the foam and it will smell deliciously nutty. This process will take 5 to 7 minutes. Remove from the heat and allow to cool slightly. In a medium bowl, stir together the eggs, sugar, maple syrup, whipping cream, salt, raisins and pecan pieces. Stream the mixture into the warm browned butter, whisking constantly. Place back over medium heat and bring to a gentle boil. Cook for 3 minutes and remove from the heat. Stir in the vanilla. Remove the tart shells from the freezer and fill two-thirds full with the tart filling. Bake for 18 to 20 minutes, or until the tart shells are lightly browned. Allow to cool and then remove from the pans. Store in an airtight container in the fridge for 4 to 5 days or for several weeks in the freezer. Thaw frozen tarts before serving and warm slightly in the oven.

Note: Feel free to swap out different nuts and/or leave out the raisins to suit your own taste buds.

linzer cookies with homemade jam

One of my mom's greatest gifts to me was freedom in the kitchen. Freedom to make a big mess and to make mistakes! At Christmas, my sister and I helped my mom bake dozens upon dozens of treats. Of course, there were always lots of cookies! Linzer cookies are as eye-catching as they are delicious.

Yield: 24 sandwich cookies

1 cup (115 g) whole hazelnuts

⅔ cup (132 g) granulated sugar

¾ cup (170 g) unsalted butter, room temperature

1 tbsp (6 g) lemon zest (about 1 lemon)

2 large egg yolks

¾ tsp ground cinnamon

¼ tsp salt

½ tsp baking powder

2 cups (250 g) all-purpose flour

Powdered sugar, as needed

1 cup (108 g) Homemade Raspberry and Rose Jam (page 202) or store-bought jam

Seasonal Substitutes

Use any type of jam or citrus curd you'd like!

Place the hazelnuts onto a rimmed baking sheet and bake for 8 to 10 minutes, stirring once or twice, until the nuts are lightly toasted. Remove and cool slightly before using. In a food processor or high-powered blender, combine the hazelnuts and sugar. Pulse until the nuts are finely ground. In the bowl of a stand mixer fitted with the paddle attachment, add the nut-sugar mixture, the butter and lemon zest. Mix on medium for 2 to 3 minutes, or until light and creamy. Add the egg yolks one at a time and mix on medium until incorporated.

In a medium bowl, whisk together the cinnamon, salt, baking powder and flour. Add the dry ingredients to the wet and mix on low until the dough pulls away from the sides of the bowl and forms a ball. Remove from the bowl and divide into two pieces. Flatten each half into a disk about 1 inch (2.5 cm) thick, wrap in plastic wrap and transfer to the fridge to chill for 30 to 40 minutes, or until the dough can be rolled out.

Preheat the oven to 350°F (180°C) while the dough is chilling. Line two 10 x 15–inch (25 x 38–cm) baking sheets with parchment or silicone baking mats.

Remove one chilled disk from the fridge and roll out onto a lightly floured surface. If the dough is too stiff and cracking quite a bit, wait 5 to 10 minutes and try again. Roll out to about ⅛ inch (3 mm) thick and use a 2½- to 3-inch (6- to 8-cm) round cookie cutter to cut out as many cookies as you can. Transfer to the prepared baking sheet. Bake for 10 to 12 minutes, or until the edges of the cookies are just starting to lightly brown. Remove from the oven and cool for a few minutes before transferring to a cooling rack. Repeat with remaining disk of dough, but cut out the centers of these cookies as they will become the top cookie in the linzer sandwich. Use traditional linzer cookie cutters to cut out the centers or simply use a slightly smaller cookie cutter. Transfer the cookie tops to the second prepared pan. Bake for 9 to 11 minutes, or until lightly brown. The top cookies usually need slightly less time compared to the bottom cookies, which is why I prefer to keep the pans separate.

Gather any scraps of dough, chill, re-roll and repeat the above steps until all the dough has been used. Once all the cookies are cool, dust all of the top cookies with powdered sugar. Spread about a tablespoon (7 g) of jam onto the bottom cookie, leaving a slight border so it doesn't ooze out. Place a top cookie over it and press down gently. Serve immediately or store in an airtight container in the fridge for several days. Cookies freeze well, either filled or unfilled.

jam-filled sweet rolls

As winter is the slowest season on the farm, it means more hours in the day for longer baking projects, with bread being one of our favorites. These sweet rolls are layered around homemade jam from summer's bounty and are easily customized to suit your fancy. Just be warned, it can get a little messy if your jam isn't super thick. But it's worth it! Want a sweet breakfast? Simply pop these rolls into the fridge before their second rise and then bake them in the morning.

Yield: 12 sweet rolls

DOUGH

¼ cup (60 ml) hot water

2¼ tsp (7 g) active dry yeast

¼ cup (50 g) granulated sugar, divided

⅓ cup (75 g) unsalted butter

¾ cup (180 ml) milk

3½–4 cups (438–500 g) all-purpose flour, divided

½ tsp salt

1 large egg

To activate the yeast, in a small bowl, add the hot (but not boiling) water, yeast and 1 tablespoon (15 g) of the granulated sugar. Stir together and set aside to rise. If this mixture doesn't froth up in 5 minutes, try again. Or you may need fresher yeast!

To make the dough, in a small saucepan, melt the butter and milk on medium heat, stirring constantly. Remove from the heat once melted and allow to cool slightly. In the bowl of a stand mixer fitted with the paddle attachment, add the remaining sugar, 2 cups (250 g) of the flour and salt. Stir in the yeast mixture and egg and mix well on medium. Then switch to low and slowly stream in the warm milk and butter mixture.

Switch to the dough hook attachment, add 1 cup (125 g) of the flour and allow the dough to come together while mixing on low. Add more flour, a few tablespoons at a time, until the dough pulls away from the sides of the bowl but is still tacky to the touch. You may not use the entire ½ cup (63 g) of the remaining flour. Mix on low for 8 minutes or knead by hand for about 10 minutes. Resist the urge to add more flour to make it perfectly smooth. A tacky dough is exactly right. Move the dough into a greased mixing bowl, cover with a clean kitchen towel and place in a warm spot to rise for 1 hour. When the dough has doubled in size, roll it out into an approximately 9 x 12–inch (23 x 30–cm) rectangle. (Hint: The pan you'll be placing them in is 9 x 13 inches [23 x 33 cm] in case you need an idea of measurements.) Let the dough rest for a few minutes.

(continued)

FILLING

¾ cup (245 g) thick jam (the thicker the better as a runny jam will not work well here)

1 cup (220 g) packed brown sugar

CREAM CHEESE FROSTING

1 cup (232 g) cream cheese, room temperature

½ cup (114 g) unsalted butter, room temperature

2 cups (240 g) powdered sugar

1 tsp vanilla extract

1 tbsp (15 ml) milk, plus more as needed

½ tbsp (3 g) lemon zest (about ½ lemon)

Pinch of salt

To make the filling, in a small bowl, stir together the jam and brown sugar. Spread the mixture over the rolled-out dough in an even layer, leaving a ¼-inch (6-mm) border along each side to help avoid the filling spilling out. With the long side of the dough closest to you, start rolling the dough into a log. Try to lift and turn rather than just pushing the dough ahead when you're rolling it. This will help avoid pushing the jam filling out too much. Pinch the seam where the log ends so that it won't come apart. Now, this part can get a little messy, so don't be scared! Use a sharp, serrated knife to cut the log in half, and then cut each half into 6 equal pieces about 1 inch (2.5 cm) wide. I will often use floss instead of a knife. You simply slide the floss under the dough, bring each piece up, cross over each other and cut. (Just make sure to use unflavored floss!) If my log is a little uneven, I'll trim each end off to straighten it and bake the extra pieces in a mini pan to help the rest of the buns stay more even! Arrange the 12 buns on a greased 9 x 13–inch (23 x 33–cm) pan. Cover with a clean dish towel and allow to rise for 20 minutes in a warm place.

Preheat the oven to 375°F (190°C) while the dough is rising.

Bake for 25 to 30 minutes, or until the tops are a deep golden brown. Place onto a wire cooling rack and let cool slightly before frosting and serving. While the rolls are cooling, prepare the frosting. In the bowl of a stand mixer fitted with the paddle attachment, beat together the cream cheese and butter until smooth. Add the powdered sugar, vanilla, milk, lemon zest and salt. Mix on medium-low until smooth. Add more milk as needed until the desired consistency is reached.

The rolls are best served warm, topped with a generous swirl of frosting. To store, keep the rolls and frosting in airtight containers in the fridge for up to 1 week, and warm slightly before serving. Rolls may also be frozen, either frosted or unfrosted, in an airtight container for a couple of months.

pie crusts

Flour, fat, water and salt. A dash of vinegar to help keep things tender. A sprinkle of sugar to add some sweetness. Some days I'll use 100 percent butter purely for the flavor, but most times I'll do half butter/half lard (or shortening). If I'm doing a lot of braiding or delicate crust work, I prefer lard as it doesn't melt as quickly as butter, which makes working with the dough easier. There's really no wrong combo though, so pick what works best for your tastes!

pie dough

My top tips for pie crust are to keep things nice and cold and stop adding water and mixing before you think it's quite done. As with anything, practice makes perfect!

Yield: crust for 1 double-crust pie or 2 single-crust pies

1 tbsp (15 ml) white vinegar

7 tbsp (105 ml) cold water

2½ cups (313 g) all-purpose flour

1 tsp salt

½ tsp baking powder

2 tbsp (28 g) brown sugar

½ cup (114 g) unsalted butter, cold

½ cup (103 g) lard (substitute with shortening or butter)

Note: If you are planning to do braiding and/or fancy decorating with leaves, etc., I suggest you make a double batch, split it into four disks and store any extra dough for a galette later on. You never want to run out of dough when you've put in a lot of work making the crust look great!

Place the vinegar in a liquid measuring cup. Fill with the cold water until you have ½ cup (120 ml) of liquid. Move to the freezer to chill while you prepare the rest of the dough. In a large bowl, whisk together the flour, salt, baking powder and brown sugar until completely combined. Set aside.

On a cutting board, chop the butter and lard into ½-inch (1.3-cm) cubes. Add the butter and lard to the flour mixture, tossing with your hands to coat. Use a pastry cutter or a fork to start cutting in the fat. When about half the butter and lard is about pea-size (some will be smaller, some will be larger), move to work with your hands. Press the larger pieces of butter and lard between your hands to create shards. I like to get my hands right in there at the end to break up any remaining large pieces while avoiding cutting the other pieces too small. Once all of the fat is roughly pea-size or in shards, move the bowl to the freezer for about 5 minutes.

Remove both the dry dough and the measuring cup with the water-vinegar mixture from the freezer. Add ¼ cup (60 ml) of the water-vinegar to the flour mixture, pouring evenly over the top. Use a wooden spoon or a spatula to gently mix the dough together. Once the dough is in a shaggy mass, dump onto the counter. Yes, it'll be messy! No, it won't quite look like dough yet. Carefully gather the outside shaggy edges and crumbs up and over the top of the dough and press down. Turn and repeat until the dough starts to come together. If the dough seems too dry and isn't coming together, carefully add a couple more teaspoons of water-vinegar mixture as you work. Try to work the dough as little as possible, otherwise it'll be tough. We don't want the dough to be perfectly smooth though, so resist the urge to add too much water. Once the dough can hold together, it's ready to go. If you ever get tacky dough, it is overhydrated, so add a bit more flour and hope for the best.

Cut the dough in half, and shape each half into a disk that's about 1 inch (2.5 cm) thick and either wrap up tightly using plastic wrap or place in a small glass container with a tight fitting lid. Let it rest and chill in the fridge for at least 1 hour or preferably overnight before rolling out. Unbaked pie dough can be frozen in an airtight container for up to 3 months. Simply thaw in your refrigerator before using.

Variations:

Substitute half the amount of all-purpose flour for either spelt flour, rye flour or buckwheat flour. You may need an extra tablespoon (15 ml) of water.

creating a lattice crust

Set a large baking sheet beside your workspace. This will be for transferring each dough strip for easy handling and can be transferred to the fridge as you work if the dough starts getting warm. Remove a disk of pie dough from the fridge and roll it out to about the same size as the bottom crust, about 2 to 3 inches (5 to 8 cm) larger than the outer edge of the pie dish. Use a sharp knife and a ruler or a pizza cutter to cut long strips. Wide or narrow, all the same size or varied—have fun with the lattice strips! Place each strip onto the baking sheet as you go, and move to the fridge if the dough warms up, as needed. Gather up any scraps that are left and roll them out again so you can cut more strips. You may need to pop these scraps into the fridge to chill a bit before you can work with them again.

1. Assemble the pie. Pour the filling into the chilled bottom crust.

2. Place the longest strip you have over the exact center of the pie.

3. Add strips on either side of it with equal spacing. Three thick strips are great if this is your first pie, and many small strips are fun to try as you gain experience.

4. Flip every other strip in half, folding over themselves.

5. Then place another long strip in the center of the pie at a 90-degree angle to the first strip(s). The dough should not crack when folded over itself. If it does, it is too cold and will need to warm up a bit before proceeding. If cracking occurs, simply press the dough back together.

6. Fold the strip(s) back down.

7. Flip the remaining strips up and over themselves.

8. Lay down another dough strip at a 90-degree angle.

9. Fold the strips back down.

10. Feel free to swap some of the strips for braids to add interest, and play around with the angles of crossovers, too.

11. Repeat this process if necessary to cover the filling, remembering to fold back alternating strips before laying a new strip of dough down. Repeat for the remaining half of the pie. When finished, each strip should alternate going over and under the strips that cross it. This will become more obvious as you work. Place the entire pie into the fridge or freezer before finishing the final edge if the dough seems to be getting too soft.

12. Trim each of the top strips so that they meet the edge of the pie dish but don't hang over much.

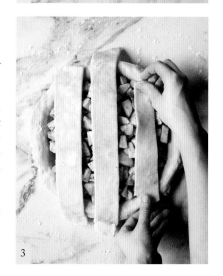

1

2

3

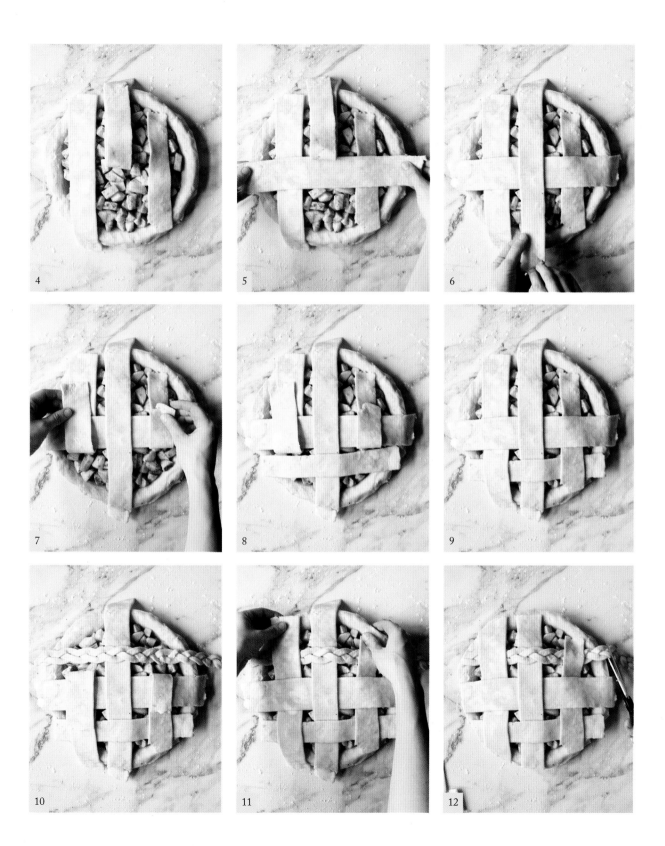

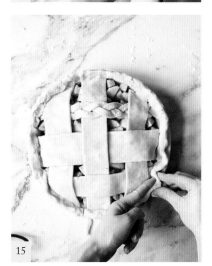

13. Fold the bottom crust layer up and over the strips, and press together.

14. Dip your fingers in a bit of water and wet the dough wherever it needs to be pressed together to help it hold firm.

15. To crimp the crust, place the thumb and index finger of one hand against the outside edge of the crust. Use the pointer finger of the other hand to press the dough outwards, between the initial thumb and finger.

Repeat along the entire border of the crust.

Alternatively, use a fork to press the dough firmly together along the edge. Place the pie in the freezer for 15 to 20 minutes, or until the dough is very firm. Brush with egg wash, sprinkle with coarse sugar and bake.

Note: The double-crust pie recipe can be used to make a simple lattice, but there won't be much dough left. I prefer to make 1½ or 2 batches of the basic pie dough recipe to ensure I won't run out!

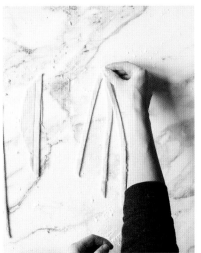

how to braid pie dough

Line a baking sheet with parchment paper and set aside. This will be for the dough braids to be placed on and transferred to the fridge or freezer if the dough gets too soft. Roll out a disk of pie dough into a long rectangle about ⅛ inch (3 mm) thick. Rolling the dough into a rectangle gives the braid strands more length, making it easier to work without patching on more length.

Use a ruler and pizza cutter to cut long strips of equal length, or use a multi-wheeled pastry cutter if you have one. Braid strand width can be varied depending on what look you are going for. I prefer thinner braids for the border crust, but I will use larger braids if making a thick lattice pie. Adding in one or two braids into a lattice crust adds fun interest and is a favorite of mine.

Once the dough has been cut, gently separate three strands.

Lightly wet the ends farthest from your body with a bit of water and press firmly together.

To braid, I simply move the center strand to the outside over the left strand and then the new center strand to the outside over the right strand.

Repeat this process as tight as you can, adding more dough to the ends if needed for length by wetting with a bit of water and pressing the new strip firmly onto the original strip.

Transfer the braid to the prepared pan and move to the fridge while you work on the next braid. If, at any point, the dough becomes too soft to work with, transfer the dough to the fridge for a few minutes to firm up. Warm dough is your worst enemy when trying to create intricate crusts.

For the Peach-Raspberry-Ginger Pie (page 93), you will need five braids to reach across the pie: one 9 inches (23 cm) long, two 8 inches (20 cm) long, two 6 inches (15 cm) long and one to circle around the edge that's about 29 inches (74 cm) long. You will likely need to re-roll and chill the scraps of dough as you work.

Once all the braids are done, remove the pie dish with the bottom crust from the fridge and add the filling. Next, start to lay out the braids. Place the 9-inch (23-cm) braid right across the center and then add the remaining braids on either side. Trim all of the braid ends to match the edge of the pie plate and press firmly into the crust. Wet the outside edge of the pie with a bit of water and carefully lay out the long braid along it, pressing gently to attach. When you reach the end of the braid, carefully tuck the end strands under the beginning of the braid. If it's too hard to make seamless, you can always cut a heart, leaf or peach shape out of the remaining dough and add it on top as a decoration and to cover the seam. Transfer the pie to the freezer for 15 to 20 minutes, or until the dough is completely firm. Bake as directed.

preserving the seasons

Savoring produce while it's at its peak is a wonderful thing; however, sometimes you may want to prolong special flavors for a little while longer. From infusing sugar with a delicate floral touch to pureeing pumpkins once they've served their decorative purpose, these preserves let us enjoy the magic of each season for just a little while longer.

lilac sugar

Lilac season may be fleeting, but this sugar lets you enjoy them for a little while longer. Sweet and floral, this sugar is quick to make and will last for the whole year. Use in place of regular sugar whenever you'd like. It works best when added to mild-flavored things so its delicate flavor is not overpowered.

Yield: about 2¼ cups (425 g)

2 cups (400 g) granulated sugar

1–2 cups (20–40 g) loosely packed lilac petals, removed from stem

Note: Lilacs are edible but always make sure that you are only picking them from your own plants that you know are safe to eat from.

Sterilize a glass jar. Preheat the oven to 200°F (95°C). Line a small baking sheet with aluminum foil and set aside. Wash a 3-cup (720-ml) or larger glass jar with soap and hot water and rinse it but don't dry it. Place it upside down on the baking sheet and bake in the oven for 10 minutes. Make sure it is completely dry before adding the sugar.

Remove each lilac flower from its green stem before using. In the sterilized jar, place ½ cup (50 g) of sugar and then layer about one-quarter of the lilac petals. Repeat 3 times. Place the lid on the jar and keep in a cool, dark place for 5 to 10 days to let the flavor infuse. Be sure to shake the jar once or twice a day to help ensure the blossoms are distributed through the sugar.

After day 5, open the jar to test the flavor strength. You may leave the jar to infuse for a few more days or add more lilac blossoms, if desired. Lilac petals are edible and may be left in the jar, or you may choose to strain them out once you are happy with the flavor of the sugar.

Note: The sugar may absorb a bit of moisture from the lilacs and become lumpy. I simply spread it on a baking tray and bake for 5 to 10 minutes at 200°F (95°C) to remove the moisture, and then return it to the airtight jar for storing.

elderflower cordial

I find elderflower cordial so therapeutic to make. Picking the large sprays of delicate, star-shaped flowers on a beautiful sunny morning is so much fun. Bring them home to use right away, pluck each flower off its stem and combine with lemon to steep for a day or two until the cordial is strong enough for your tastes. It almost feels like magic. Elderflower cordial can be used in many desserts, but is also delicious when added to fizzy water for a perfectly refreshing summer drink. Pick your elderflower sprays fresh if you can, but always make sure you are 100 percent certain about your plant identification, or find a farm that does u-pick. You'll need three 17-ounce (500-ml) glass bottles with lids and a metal funnel.

Yield: 3 (17-oz [500-ml]) bottles

2 cups (50 g) loosely packed elderflowers, plucked from their stem

4 cups (960 ml) water

3 cups (600 g) granulated sugar

1 tbsp (6 g) lemon zest (about 1 lemon)

2 tbsp (30 ml) fresh lemon juice (about 1 lemon), retain the lemon halves

Note: Pick the elderflower sprays early in the morning on a sunny day and make the cordial immediately if you can. If you need to store the sprays, pluck them off the stem, place on a baking sheet, cover with a slightly damp paper towel and keep them in the fridge.

Note: To extend the storage life of the cordial, you can add 1 tablespoon (14 g) of citric acid to the sugar.

If using fresh elderflowers, shake off the flowers before using to remove any small insects that may be hanging out. I don't recommend washing them if you can help it, as the water will wash away most of the pollen, which carries the flavor. Set the flowers aside.

In a large saucepan or Dutch oven, bring the water to a boil and stir in the sugar until dissolved. Boil for 2 to 3 minutes, and then remove from the heat and allow to cool slightly. Add the lemon zest and juice and cut up the remaining lemon halves into chunks and add those, too. Stir in the elderflowers. Cover the pot, transfer to the fridge and leave for 24 to 36 hours to infuse the flavors.

When the mixture is ready, sterilize three 17-ounce (500-ml) glass bottles. Preheat the oven to 200°F (95°C). Line a small baking sheet with aluminum foil and set aside. Wash the glass bottles and a metal funnel with soap and hot water and rinse them but skip drying them. Place everything on the baking sheet and bake in the oven for 10 minutes. Turn the oven off, but leave the jars in the oven to stay warm until ready to use. They don't need to be completely dry before you use them. Place the lids in a small saucepan and fill with enough water to cover them. Bring to a gentle simmer and cook for about 10 minutes. Turn off the heat and leave the jars in the water until ready to use.

Remove the lemon chunks from the pot and squeeze them into the cordial to get all the flavor and liquid out. Discard the lemon chunks. Strain the remaining cordial through a fine-mesh sieve or a piece of clean muslin cloth. Place the liquid into a large, clean saucepan and bring to a gentle boil for 4 to 5 minutes. Remove the warm, sterilized bottles and funnel from the oven, and use the funnel to add the cordial to each bottle, dividing between the three evenly. Never pour hot liquid into a cool glass bottle as this could cause the bottle to crack. Allow the cordial to cool to room temperature before closing the bottles and transferring them to the fridge. For longer storage, freeze the cordial in a freezer-safe, straight-sided jar (no shoulders and leave at least ½ inch [1.3 cm] of headspace for expansion).

homemade raspberry and rose jam

One of the best tricks my mom taught me is to freeze a bag (or five!) of berries during the summer and wait until winter to make jam with them. Any smooshy berries I won't use before going bad go into the bag, sometimes even getting squished down to make more room as I pack them in. Then, in winter, when I don't mind standing over a hot stove, I'll pull them out and make jam! Raspberry jam is my favorite, and it is so simple to cook up. I prefer to store mine in the freezer and will skip the canning part of the process, but you're welcome to do so if you'd rather store them in your pantry. I added a few drops of rose water for an interesting twist, but you could substitute orange blossom water or vanilla if you'd prefer. You'll need three straight-sided canning jars with lids, and a wide-mouth funnel will be helpful but not necessary.

Yield: 3 cups (325 g)

5½ cups (676 g) fresh or frozen raspberries

2 cups (400 g) granulated sugar

¼–¾ tsp rose water

Note: You cannot store this jam at room temperature unless it's properly canned in a water bath.

Sanitize the jam jars and a metal funnel. Preheat the oven to 200°F (95°C). Line a small rimmed baking sheet with aluminum foil. Wash the jars with soapy water and rinse the funnel thoroughly, skip the drying and set them on the baking sheet. Bake for 10 minutes, turn off the oven and leave the jars in the oven to stay warm until ready to use. Place the lids in a small saucepan and fill with enough water to cover them. Bring to a gentle simmer and cook for about 10 minutes. Turn off the heat and leave the jars in the water until ready to use. Place a small plate into your freezer. This will be used when you test your jam's doneness.

In a large heavy-bottomed pot (go bigger than you think you should, as the jam will really bubble!), stir together the raspberries and sugar. Heat over medium-high heat, stirring constantly, and bring the mixture to a boil. Once the mixture is at a boil where the bubbles don't disappear when you stir, cook for 5 minutes, until it starts to thicken. To test if it's done, place a small spoonful of jam onto the plate in the freezer and check on it after 20 to 30 seconds to see if it's thick! If yes, then you're good to go and can remove the jam from the heat. If not, keep cooking for a few more minutes. Once removed from the heat, stir in the rose water, to taste. If you are choosing to use a canning method to preserve your jam, you can seal the jars and proceed with canning at this point.

Remove the sterilized jars from the oven, place the sterilized funnel over the first jar and fill with jam. Leave at least ½ inch (1.3 cm) of headroom at the top of the jar. Repeat with the remaining jars. Place the lids onto the jars, but don't tighten them all the way. Let the jam cool to room temperature before moving to the fridge. Once chilled, tighten the lids all the way, and transfer the jars to the freezer until ready to use (label and date your containers!). They will keep for 1 year in the freezer and about 2 months, once open, in the fridge. Thaw in the fridge overnight before using.

pumpkin puree

Homemade pumpkin puree simply tastes better. Although, technically, any variety of pumpkin will work, please make sure to buy a proper cooking pumpkin so that the flavor is sweet and the texture is smooth! One of the most common questions we get on the farm is, "Which pumpkins are best for baking with?" I'll spare you the essay, but I love telling people that most of the colorful heirloom varieties are actually fantastic to bake with. Cinderella, Blue Doll, Porcelain Doll, Galeux d'Eysines' (Peanut pumpkin!), Long Island Cheese, Autumn Buckskin and Fairytale are all great choices, just to name a few! Use them to decorate your front porch (or in my case, fill my apartment), and then cook them up and freeze the puree for future baking projects. Looking for something smaller and easier to handle? Try Sugar or Baby Pam pumpkins, both small, sweet orange pumpkins. I personally don't recommend picking out a regular jack-o'-lantern pumpkin for baking with as its flavor can be quite bland. Freeze pumpkin puree in 1- or 2-cup (240- or 480-ml) portions and enjoy it all year long!

Yield: depends on size of pumpkin

Cooking spray or butter, for greasing

1 cooking pumpkin (Ask your local farmer about varieties if you can! My faves: Sugar, Baby Pam, Cinderella and Peanut)

Preheat the oven to 375°F (190°C). Line a large baking sheet with aluminum foil, grease with cooking spray or butter and set aside.

Wash the pumpkin thoroughly and dry it before starting. Break off the stem.

For smaller pumpkins, use a large knife to cut it in half. For large pumpkins, I will often stick the point of the knife into the top where the stem was, pointing down to the table, and then slowly push the handle down to safely cut.

You can also use a small paring knife or peeler to carve a groove into the pumpkin first so that your knife won't slip if the skin of the pumpkin is extra tough to get through. Repeat this cutting motion to cut a wedge of pumpkin off, similar to how you would cut a piece of pie.

Depending on the size of your pumpkin, cut into quarters, or again into eighths. For very large pumpkins, you may want to cut the slices down even more. Each slice shouldn't be much wider than your hand, otherwise it will take longer to cook. Try to keep the slices fairly even, so that they will be done at the same time. Use a spoon to scrape along the center flesh, pulling out the seeds and stringy bits in the middle.

Rinse the seeds immediately and keep them for later if you want to roast them. Place each pumpkin slice flesh down onto the prepared pan and roast in the oven for 45 to 60 minutes.

(continued)

pumpkin puree (continued)

Flip the pumpkin slices a couple times while roasting, keeping the flesh side down. If the slices appear to be getting a bit dry, you can add a small amount of hot water to the pan. This helps keep things moist and soft. The pumpkin is done when a fork easily pierces the flesh. If in doubt, leave it in for a bit longer!

Remove from the oven when done and allow to cool for 10 to 15 minutes before handling again—it will be hot! Small pumpkins often have very soft skins and don't need to be peeled. For thicker skin, use a spoon to scrape along the skin, scooping all of the inner flesh out.

Transfer the pumpkin flesh into a blender or food processor, or use an immersion blender to blend until smooth. You may need to scrape down the sides and give it a stir before blending again.

Place the puree into a fine-mesh sieve (cheesecloth would work, too), and set the sieve over a large bowl. Let it drain for at least 20 minutes before using or storing. This helps the excess water drain away, and drainage time will vary depending on the pumpkin variety. I find that this helps me control the consistency of the puree better compared to what you find in a store (and what is used in most recipes).

You should have smooth and creamy puree that is ready to be used in any pumpkin recipe your heart desires. Store in the fridge for a few days if you're going to use it within 1 week or freeze it in 1- or 2-cup (240- or 480-ml) increments for future use. It freezes extremely well, but I'll repeat the sieve draining method once I pull the puree out of the freeze and thaw it.

Note: The color of your puree will vary slightly with the pumpkin you use, as the different types of pumpkins/squashes have varying color saturations!

rhubarb compote

As rhubarb is one of my most cherished flavors, I'm always on the lookout for ways to incorporate it into my life. This rhubarb compote is definitely a staple. I'll cook a big batch and serve it over ice cream, add it in between cake layers or frosting . . . and it makes a lovely addition to a bowl of overnight oatmeal. I find it a great way to use up extra rhubarb if I've picked too much for a pie, and it cooks up in no time.

Yield: about 2½ cups (600 ml)

3–4 medium rhubarb stalks

¾–1 cup (150–200 g) granulated sugar

2 tbsp (30 ml) water

1 tsp vanilla extract

Chop the rhubarb into ½-inch (1.3-cm) cubes. Place it in a saucepan with the sugar and water and heat on medium, stirring occasionally, until the rhubarb has broken down and forms a thick, relatively smooth compote. This will take about 15 to 20 minutes. You may want to mash the rhubarb down about halfway through the cooking time to help move it along. Remove the compote from the heat once it is thick and jammy. Stir in the vanilla and allow it to cool to room temperature. Transfer the compote to an airtight container and store in the fridge for up to 3 weeks.

Note: The amount of sugar and rhubarb used is highly subjective to personal taste. I always prefer my rhubarb compote to be a bit tart, especially when paired with a sweet cake. Taste and adjust yours as you see fit! It's much easier to add more sugar than to add too much and have it too sweet.

lemon curd

Lemon curd is a great addition to ice cream, cakes, whipped cream or even to eat on toast. I like mine pretty zippy, especially if it's served with a sweet dessert. It takes so little time to whip up, and I love having a little jar in my fridge to add some brightness to my treats, especially during the dark and dreary winter months. Try swapping the lemon for other types of citrus, too!

Yield: 1⅓ cups (320 ml)

½ cup (120 ml) fresh lemon juice (about 3–4 lemons)

1 tbsp (6 g) lemon zest (about 1 lemon)

½ cup (100 g) granulated sugar, or more or less depending on desired tartness level

4 large egg yolks

½ cup (114 g) cubed salted butter

Place a fine-mesh sieve over a heatproof bowl and set aside.

In a medium nonreactive saucepan (stainless steel or enamel works well), combine the lemon juice, zest, sugar, egg yolks and butter and heat on medium-low. Whisk continuously to keep the eggs from cooking separately. Cook the mixture until it starts to thicken and the whisk starts leaving trails, about 10 minutes. The curd should be done when the first bubble appears on the surface and has reached 170°F (77°C). If it has not thickened after 10 minutes, simply turn the heat up slightly and keep cooking. Remove from the heat and strain through the fine-mesh sieve to remove any stray egg yolks, if necessary, and to remove the lemon zest for a perfectly smooth curd. Allow to cool to room temperature before transferring to an airtight container in the fridge. Place a layer of plastic wrap on top of the curd to keep a film from forming, if desired. Keep refrigerated until ready to serve. The curd will keep up to 1 week in the fridge or up to 1 year in the freezer.

Variations:

Use grapefruit or lime in place of the lemon for different flavors of curd!

Note: Using a reactive saucepan such as aluminum or unlined copper can cause the acid from the lemons to discolor and have an unappetizing metallic taste, so be sure to use a nonreactive saucepan and utensils. Stainless steel or enameled cookware are good choices.

freezing fruit

Freezing fruit may seem like common sense, but I'm always amazed by how many questions I get about it. Plums in particular seem to blow people's minds, mostly because they've never thought to freeze them, I suppose! Most fruits freeze well, and I love stocking up on local fruit when it's in season and freezing a little extra for the coming months.

For All Fruit

Rinse and let air-dry on towels before freezing. Once the fruit is totally dry, lay it in a single layer onto the largest baking sheets that will fit in your freezer and freeze for a few hours until solid. Move the fruit to airtight containers for long-term storage.

Berries

Most can be frozen whole, although I recommend hulling and halving strawberries. Blueberries can usually skip the freezing on a baking sheet step, and I often freeze them right in their container. This works unless they're overripe or mushy, as that can cause them to freeze into a solid block.

Cherries

Remove the stems and pit.

Stone Fruit

Peel, if necessary, and then halve, pit and slice into quarters (or smaller slices, if desired). Toss with a bit of lemon juice to keep from browning before laying out on baking sheets.

acknowledgments

To the readers and supporters of The Farmer's Daughter, thank you.

This book would never have happened if I hadn't decided to pick up a camera ten years ago to document my baking adventures, in a move greatly inspired by Joy from Joy the Baker and Heather from Sprinkle Bakes. Thank you to all the bloggers who came before me, providing inspiration throughout the years. It's an honor to be part of such a kind and talented community.

To the supportive team at Page Street, thank you for holding my hand throughout this process and for believing that I had a unique story to tell.

To my friends near and far who I badgered constantly with recipe samples, photos to choose between, cover options and more. Thank you for your advice, your cheerleading and for never making me feel *too* needy: Jordyn, Jorica, Jen, Kristie, Clara, Jenna and Courtney.

To the abundance of farms and markets in Abbotsford, the Fraser Valley and Okanagan. I am truly blessed to have access to such amazing produce and am beyond grateful that "eating local" is becoming such a celebrated thing.

To our farm, Willow View Farms, for the influence growing up on a farm has had on my life and the way I bake, and for providing apples, pumpkins, squash, saskatoons and so much more for this book.

To my roommate, Courtney, thank you for your endless patience with my kitchen messes (and for all the times you cleaned up after me), your enthusiasm for trying each new treat and for helping keep our freezer stash to a reasonable volume by letting me send desserts with you to work.

To Amy, thank you for letting me ask you a million questions about the book-writing process, for not murdering me during our first in-person meeting-turned-cake-baking-sleepover-weekend, and for being a constant inspiration.

To Clara, thank you for believing in me and my creativity and voice long before I did. Thank you for the hours you spent recipe testing, giving me pep talks and relentlessly supporting me every step of the way.

To Jorica, thank you for the hours you spent reading through each recipe, for checking in on me when things got a little rocky and for your thoughtfulness.

To my dad, for never tiring of the endless supply of desserts I brought over for you to try, and for the consistently honest feedback when "It kind of looks like marinating meat instead of bread."

To my mom, for first teaching me to bake, giving me space to make mistakes of my own and for encouraging me to always follow my dreams.

To Jordyn, my favorite (and only) sister. Thank you for always being there to lend a listening ear whenever I had a meltdown, for washing ten million dishes for me on the weekends and for eagerly trying out each new recipe. I couldn't have done this without you.

about the author

Kelsey Siemens is a food photographer and the creator of The Farmer's Daughter, a baking blog that features approachable desserts influenced by her life on the farm. She has been featured in *Bake from Scratch*, *Country Sampler*, *Good Housekeeping* and more. She lives in Abbotsford, BC, Canada, where she continues to work and find inspiration on her family's apple and pumpkin farm.

index